THE INSIDIOUS DANCE

The Paralysis of Perfectionism

Jim Banks

Author of
The Effects of Trauma and How to Deal with It
Defeating Jezebel
One Calling, One Ministry

House of Healing Ministries

P.O. Box 60 Campbellsville, KY 42719
www.houseohealingministries.org
www.traumaprayer.com

email: office@houseofhealingministries.org
phone: 828-273-1249
1st Printing 2013

All scripture quotations, unless otherwise noted, are taken from the Holy Bible, Authorized King James Version, Public Domain, or from the Revised Standard Version of the Bible, copyright 1952 [2nd edition, 1971] by the Division of Christian Education of the National Council of the Churches of Christ in the United States of America. Scripture quotations marked (NKJV) are taken from the New King James Version. Copyright 1982, Thomas Nelson, used by permission. All Rights Reserved.

Please note that House of Healing Ministries publishing style capitalizes certain pronouns in Scripture that refer to the Father, Son, and Holy Spirit and may differ from some Bible publishers' style.

Please note that the name satan and any related names are purposely not capitalized. We choose not to acknowledge him even to the point of violating grammatical rules.

© Copyright 2013 – House of Healing Ministries.
All Rights Reserved. No part of this book may be reproduced in any form, except for the inclusions of brief quotations in review, without expressed written permission by the author/publisher.

Printed in the U.S.A.

About the Author

Jim Banks' formal training was in electrical engineering. He served as an electrical design engineer on industrial projects for several years. Later he moved into design work modernizing the electrical infrastructure of older buildings to provide for the needs of modern electronic devices. This technical background allowed him to make a career move into sales and marketing where he worked for several industrial manufacturers, rising to sales and marketing manager for several firms. His wife, Pat, worked as a trainer for Southwestern Bell for many years. Together they have four children and six grandchildren. They entered the inner-healing ministry over twenty-five years ago, initially on a part-time basis.

Operating out of a local church, Jim and Pat established a healing community in Asheville, NC, in 2005. That community continues to offer a broad range of classes, support groups, individual sessions, and therapies which are able to help an individual walk through just about any situation where emotional and spiritual problems have created unresolved painful issues, broken relationships, and daily dysfunctionality.

Jim and Pat are also the founders of House of Healing Ministries, currently operating in Campbellsville, KY. Through their vision casting, teaching, and mentoring, they have helped establish dozens of healing rooms and healing communities across the nation. They have trained over 6,000 people in some phase of physical and emotional healing in the last five years alone.

Their hearts' desire is to raise up numerous comprehensive, lay-led healing communities wrapped around one or more local congregations to serve their local community with the healing hand of Jesus. One of their efforts is to offer multiple events around the country, their "Inner Healing & Deliverance RoundTables and Symposiums," through which they introduce various inner healing and deliverance modalities and programs that contribute to a comprehensive healing community.

They also offer private personal prayer ministry by appointment.

P.O. Box 60
Campbellsville. KY 42719
828.273.1249

This is dedicated to those of you who are looking for a way out of the MATRIX, to escape from the system of the world and experience all that life has to offer. This may just be the right pill to swallow.

Introduction

I am, as are many of you, an ardent observer of human behavior and I am always curious as to why people think the way they do and behave in the manner that they do. I suppose I came by it honestly when my mother first spanked me for falling out of a tree—not because I was climbing it without permission, or in rebellion against a local tree climbing ordinance, but because it scared her. What was up with that? Why would that be a problem?

My wife and I have been in the business of helping people get through and get over all manner of issues in the last three decades, as we simultaneously held down regular jobs and raised four kids. The latter effort was a major experiment in molding and shaping human behavior, in spite of our cluelessness about it. The jury is still out on how well we did. The last ten years of ministry haven't been much different, except that we've done it full time.

As is usual for most mental health practitioners, not that I am one by training and prefer to be known as a prayer minister, delving into the inner workings of the human mind and spirit lures oneself into progressively deeper and deeper waters in an attempt to help those who are progressively more wounded and broken than the last bunch. It is a function of human pride to believe that you can help anyone, regardless of their presenting issue, coupled with the intrigue of the search for the magic bullet that unlocks the heart and mind of the most captivated of captives.

The curious thing about my observations is that those who seem to be able to function on any level within the framework of our society, from marginal to those who excel, are all in some way emotionally handicapped by performance or perfectionism. Seemingly universally, this "disease" (and this is not a DSM-IV diagnosis) robs every one of its adherents of the very life they are so enthusiastically in pursuit of. The result is an impassioned desire to be fully alive, yet experientially they somehow find themselves disconnected from the ability to achieve it.

What you're about to dive into in this book is a look at this cultural phenomenon from two perspectives: the natural and the spiritual (1 Corinthians 15:46), but ultimately through the eyes of one who has been ministering to those with this issue for over twenty-five years. Since everything has a significant spiritual component to it, the reasons behind the drive for perfection as well as the methods behind the madness cannot be ignored. As each is unveiled, I will also attempt to provide an antidote for the cultural Kool-Aid we've all had more than just a taste of.

Understand also that this book is written from the view of a layman without the benefit of the latest sociological research and formal psychological educational background. It is strictly from the point-of-view of twenty-five plus years of first-hand experience in helping people heal the wounds and shed the restrictions that have kept them from being who they were created to be.

While I'm on that subject . . . With the result of sin and the impact of significant wounds, brokenness occurs, which is most readily recognized in the form of loss of or an inhibition in personal identity. This is always the result as people dysfunctionally try to become something or someone more acceptable, or less rejectable, less susceptible, or perhaps even impervious to pain. Effectively they become someone who is not like the real, authentic person they were meant to be. Because they have chosen to be someone or something other than what God designed them to be, they are out of alignment with His will and therefore out of a place of grace with the Father. It is little wonder that things do not go well with them; that life has become tiresome and frustrating and that fulfillment from that which they have chosen to give themselves to has eluded them.

We have to understand that **grace does not flow to woundedness or brokenness, it flows to design**.

This is not to say that God's grace is not available to us in time of great need because it is. What I am saying is that this truth explains why sometimes things are very hard – you're simply not where you're supposed to be.

Significantly broken and wounded people become increasingly unable to grasp and execute the true reason they were put on the earth. They have, therefore, lost or forfeited their real identity and purpose in exchange for something that seemed safer and more acceptable.

Consequently, the understanding that Pat and I have gained from what we've studied and the experience we have acquired from the years of one-on-one personal prayer ministry, along with the tools we've chosen to use, have culminated in the concept that what we are really doing is engaging in the process of the restoration of personal identity. Basically, it's what we do. So why not call it that?

Restoring personal identity restores personal purpose. Pursuing personal purpose restores, firmly establishes, and enables personal fulfillment.

I trust that the contents of this book will give you some valuable insight into some of the issues you've identified that you are struggling with and that it will help guide you into breaking off (and away from) many of the hindrances that have kept you (and others) from experiencing all the life you can handle.

The Symptoms

Following a "Healing Rooms" presentation in Boone, NC, a few years ago, a young woman came to me expressing her personal frustration with her seeming inability to prioritize her life. She wanted deeply to be in some form of the ministry that I was teaching on but felt that her personal intimacy with the Lord was not at an acceptable level. She was also afraid that she would get too involved and her young children would suffer. She just wasn't sure she could balance it all. I asked her a few clarifying questions about her frustration and about her understanding of the healing ministry. Nothing was added. And yet she seemed to be very unsettled by the prospect of the opportunity that was before her. This was in direct contrast to her age (late-twenties), countenance, natural beauty, and presumed financial status, as indicated by the size of the rock on her left hand accompanying the Rolex.

I asked her if she was a first-born, to which she replied "yes." I then reeled off a list of first-born traits, her eyes widening significantly with each one. I told her that in all likelihood her relationship with her father was poor to non-existent; that she lived in constant frustration bordering on anger (at which point she began to shake visibly); she had never liked the person she saw in the mirror every morning; and to cap it all off I said, *"I'll bet you've never been able to receive a compliment either, and your marriage is getting difficult"*—with that she began to cry. Then I delivered the final blow; I said, *"Your marriage is in serious difficulty because your husband has been pounding continuously at your heart's door, and you don't know how to let him in. He's really frustrated, and you're afraid that he's about to give up."* At that point, she fell into my arms, sobbing uncontrollably. The Holy Spirit had hit the nail squarely on the head, with considerable force, several times in a row.

These are just a few of the classic symptoms of an individual who has adopted perfectionism as a means to getting emotional needs met. It likely describes at least 50 percent of our populous today—and another 10 percent are unable to face their issues at all. Perfectionism causes people to live in great pain and under great stress and leaves them without a clue as to how to find relief. For many, this has become a lifestyle that causes all manner of health issues to crop up as a physical expression of their emotional misery.

A Troubling Social Phenomenon

When Toyota entered the US auto market it did so with an inexpensive compact car called the Corolla. It didn't enter the market with a full line of cars and trucks. It came with a very low end entry, which General Motors took note of but chose not to respond to strategically. GM, the world's largest manufacturer of pickup trucks, made a conscious decision to not defend the low end of their business because it was certainly not as profitable as the balance of the higher end GM offerings, of which there were plenty. As Toyota grew and established a solid reputation, they gradually began to introduce a series of larger and more expensive models. As before, GM continued to ignore them. Eventually, that head-in-the-sand competitive business philosophy led GM to the brink of disaster. The result: in mid-year 2012, GM was just emerging from US bankruptcy protection, and they had literally given up on 60 percent of the domestic automobile market. The really sad part is that when Nissan, Isuzu, Honda, Mazda, Mitsubishi, and Subaru eventually entered the US market on Toyota's heels, GM's strategy never changed.

When social scientists took a retrospective look at GM's over all responses to Toyota's successive market entries and their decided lack of response to the increasing competition, they discovered something very interesting: how we respond in our private lives is pretty much identical to how we respond in the business arena.

The massive problems with the GM business model ultimately came down to a mirror image of the manner of personal life modeled by its executives; their poor short term decisions made for horrid long term results.

This is a perfect picture of the ills of our current culture because we live in such a performance-oriented society that productivity has become the chief mark by which Americans establish their own personal validity and gain a sense of worth. Unfortunately, that urge to produce can mask other equally important life objectives. This showed itself in the lives of the families of every GM executive of the period.

In our performance-oriented society, whenever an individual has fifteen or twenty minutes to themselves to do as they wish, they resort to doing something which provides a sense of accomplishment. This element of short-term gratification is, however, just another expression of the need to be productive; hence, such activities as interacting with spouses or children (long-term investment opportunities) seldom find their way onto the list of possible options.

What happened with GM, then, is indicative of the skewed values of the world's system. If it is true that it is only our personal productivity and competency which determines our personal value then we must be consistently busy. Idle hands are the devil's workshop you know. Wonder where that came from? And yet it is that very thing, the constant activity, that robs us of the time to experience life itself, along with the relationships which have the potential to make them all the more enjoyable by the hard work we do if we make time for them.

Nearly every movie worth seeing has a significant element of human connectedness central to the story line. In the multi-million dollar action film ***Avatar***, Jake Sully (Sam

Worthington) is a paraplegic war veteran who is brought to the planet Pandora to participate in a program designed to help him walk again. The program introduces him to his avatar, a creature whose genetics are half human and half Na'vi (the native blue people who are a local humanoid race that inhabits the planet). The earthlings are hell-bent on defeating the Na'vi because they are caretakers of a planet where significant mining interests are located.

Before too long, Jake's sympathies fall with the Na'vi, and he causes his avatar to take sides with the Na'vi and ends up sacrificing himself on their behalf. The closing scene has Jake meeting face to face with his avatar's love interest. In that closing scene, as she cradles Jake in her arms, Jake looks into her eyes and says, "*I see you*," a Na'vi term of endearment.

The reality is that we have all longed for someone to be close enough to know us, to "*see who we really are.*" I don't see you mask alone; I see the real you. (Your heart) That's what this interchange was meant to convey. In that same sense, each of us is born personally longing for someone to get close enough to us that they would really appreciate the complexities of our personhood: our character (including its flaws); our strengths (while knowing our weaknesses); our virtues; morals; the things we value; what we love as well as what we hate; our abilities, talents, and skills; our sense of humor; and the way we appreciate beauty and are revolted by injustice. We want someone that will see all of the good . . . and know who we really are and accept us just as we are in spite of all our flaws and failures, and do so without judging us in the process.

And then, there's the movie **Shall We Dance?** . . .

In the 2004 movie *Shall We Dance?*, Richard Gere, Jennifer Lopez, and Susan Sarandon star in a romantic comedy where a bored, overworked estate lawyer, upon first sight of a beautiful dance instructor, signs up for ballroom dancing lessons. One scene in particular caught my attention. Gere's movie wife (Susan Sarandon) hired a private investigator to find out where her husband went every Tuesday night. When she found out it was only to dance lessons, she arranged to meet with the investigator to pay him off and end the investigation. The investigator himself has just been through an ugly separation/divorce and accuses her of being a hopeless romantic and asks, "What's the point of marriage anyway?"

Her answer has to be in the Bible somewhere because her soliloquy is nothing short of Godly wisdom. She replied to him:

> *We need a witness to our lives. There's a billion people on the planet... I mean, what does any one life really mean? But in a marriage, you're promising to care about everything. The good things, the bad things, the terrible things, the mundane things... all of it, all of the time, every day. You're saying "Your life will not go unnoticed because I will notice it. Your life will not go un-witnessed because I will be your witness."*

What an absolutely profound statement, as well as a compelling and accurate assessment of the fundamental role of marriage partners in each others life.

I've ministered to numerous men whose frequent complaint was that their dad never attended any event they ever participated in, sports or otherwise. From a purely intellectual point of view, how is it that a young man in the middle of an athletic field trying not to get run over expects to communicate meaningfully with his dad, especially when his dad in the bleachers 350 feet away trying to talk about crabgrass with a neighbor over the noise of the band and other spectators? He can't. But the fact is that every son and daughter is fully aware when the most important person in their lives is in the stands watching—and when he's not. It's all about presence. And that presence makes a very loud statement: *You are important to me! You matter!*

One of the most primitive drives of every man and woman is to be known. We all desperately want to be liked, to be appreciated, to have friends, and to be connected to people who think we are somebody special and who are happy to be around us.

Then There's My Grandfather

My paternal grandfather, despite his slender frame, was a rather imposing figure at six feet four inches, especially in the small east Texas town of Teague which had around 3,500 inhabitants during the mid-to-late 50s. That was plenty tall for a skinny youngster who may have been a shade over four feet tall at the time of this particular memory. I didn't get to know him well since we didn't get to visit very often, just summers when our parents would drop me and my younger brother off while they took a brief vacation. What I heard and observed during those stays gave me the distinct impression that I knew a good deal more about him than I perhaps I thought I did. My personal experiences with him made some of the stories I heard later totally believable.

Being the oldest grandchild, I was kind of expected to accompany him to town each day to get the mail. Now, town was only three blocks away and "town" was only about three-and-a-half block long, but the trip was important for this retired former Esso pumping station manager and engineer. I knew the trip was on when he would put down his newspaper, look down, and briefly check the state of cleanliness of the white open collared shirt he always wore. Then he'd get up from his chair and head for the back door. He would stop at the hat rack to retrieve his light gray Stetson, tell my grandmother he was going to town to get the mail, give her a respectful peck on the cheek, and put on his hat—all in one seemingly fluid motion. He would say over his shoulder as he headed out the kitchen door to the garage, "*You comin?*"

We'd get into that four-door, blue and white Pontiac and back out of the dirt floored garage and roll down the windows. He'd hang a pointy elbow out the open window and off we'd go. His motion was always so fluid that he never seemed to do anything in a hurry, yet he could cover more ground than any man I've ever known. He turned to me one time, probably noting that I was scurrying to keep up, and said, "*Whenever you walk, walk with purpose, like you have to be somewhere.*" I supposed that meant "pick up the pace." That pretty much eliminated sauntering from my habits. Turns out that twenty years later a boss who was responsible for two of my major promotions said that I first came to his attention because he noted that, "*everywhere you went you walked like there was something important you had to take care of.*"

Our first stop in town was always the post office. Like so many others, this post office was built during the 30s and was still a thing of architectural beauty and reverence—lots of brass, marble and polished oak, a substantive and stately structure with lots and lots of little brass box doors all proudly lined up displaying the muted shine of their combination lock knobs and latches. But the thing I couldn't help but notice was that when my grandfather entered the building, everyone turned and acknowledged his presence verbally, *"Mr. Banks"* (with a tip of the hat of course). In turn, my grandfather would typically go round the room greeting each individual, and not like a politician or a used car salesman because he was genuinely interested in each person he engaged. Getting the mail was apparently his excuse to get out of the house and mingle a bit. Although there may have been small talk about the weather and fishing, he never stopped to make small talk for small talk's sake. He routinely asked how things were going, or inquired about someone's health, the state of a crop, or how their trip over to Waco or up to Fort Worth went.

My grandfather was a man who always faced people directly when talking to them. He was a stickler for looking people in the eye. At the time, I didn't know nor appreciate what he was doing, but invariably I would watch him stop what he was doing to move around to get where he could face someone, or even stoop a bit so he could engage an eye under a hat brim. He knew the eye was the window to the soul, and he searched as deeply as people would allow. I never saw him avoid a single person, regardless of where we went or whom we bumped into. I never heard him talk about anyone behind their back, make some snide remark about someone's character under his breath, or tell stories about the dumb things they'd done. He seemed to be genuinely interested in people and their personal welfare.

From the post office, we would walk to the hardware store, then the feed store, then to the bank or the barber shop. Same deal everywhere we went. He would always introduce me, and on occasion people would recognize me from a previous visit and ask about my parents and where they were.

The "Mr. Banks" greeting always puzzled me. I thought it was beyond the normal politeness of the time. He wasn't a local politician, a banker who held a mortgage, a doctor or druggist who knew everybody's issues, or the pastor who knew all the local dirt from years of trying to hold marriages together. And he wasn't the recipient of death-bed confessions—nothing that would give "Mr. Banks" something to hold over their heads or place him in a position of authority. My guess as to why he wanted to be so connected to people comes from a story my grandmother told me a few years after he had died.

When he and my grandmother had married, he worked for the railroad. Somewhere along the line they found themselves living and working in New Orleans during the depression on Teague Street. As was typical during that time, individuals who could not find work tried to stay alive by panhandling and begging. There were apparently a number who found their way to the back door of my grandparents' home in search of a handout. At some point, my grandfather found out that his beloved wife was turning men away, refusing the help them in their desperate hour. Angered, my aunt told me that she actually heard him scold her firmly saying, *"Don't you ever let me hear of that happening again!"*

A few years ago, my brother, sister and I were at my aunt's house, which was formerly my grandparents' home, looking at a collection of old photos. Among them were photographs of individuals I had never met, nor heard of, and yet their pictures were part of the "family collection." I asked her who these people were. She said, *"Oh that's so-and-so. Your grandparents took him in when he was thirteen or fourteen. He stayed with us until he went off to college. Over the years they took in five or six kids and helped raise them."*

I would love to have really *known* my grandparents. Life didn't provide that opportunity. Still, there were some significant glimpses provided by stories that filtered down that at least allowed me to know about what kind of people they really were. And those few experiences of "going to town" with my grandfather gave me the sense that, regardless of his place in the town as a wage-earner or his position as a deacon at the First Baptist Church, he was a man who was well respected for others and likewise held everyone else in high regard. He was a man who took the time to get to know people and a man who was vitally connected to those he lived among, and he was none too shy at demonstrating it. The assessment of the members of his community seemed to be significantly enhanced because he was honored where ever he went. As he reached out to *know*, he became *known*.

Inherent in the story lines of a failed GM business strategy, a few Hollywood blockbusters, and the life of my grandfather is the age old struggle to know and be known—the quest to become understood and appreciated and to finally settle the question *"Am I of value?"* We humans are intensely concerned with our personal identity and whether that identity makes us acceptable to people. But all too often the signals of the world, along with those most important to us, give us the distinct impression that we have somehow missed the mark. So we embark upon a process of trying to determine what is and isn't acceptable about us and, henceforth, attempt to minimize its impact in our lives.

Another point inherent in these four stories is that none of the elements that make up our lives are separate from one another. A wound, as well as attitudes, in one area affects other areas as well. Broken family relationships impact our relationships at work. Our struggles at work wind up being dragged home and are allowed to invade our family atmosphere. We naturally integrate joy, sorrow, anger, shame, and contentment almost uniformly across every area of our lives, without even thinking about it.

Every one of us who lived through elementary school can probably remember the absolute cruelty of our fellow students. During that period, we likely looked at our reflection in the mirror and could point out three or more things that we didn't like: maybe our hair was too straight or too curly or our hairline was too far back or too far forward or eyes were too big or too small ... For many of us, ever since that time, we've been trying to be someone else, someone more handsome or prettier, or someone more acceptable or funnier or ... whatever. All because we wanted to be popular and could not accept ourselves as we were. This is the root of perfectionism and all its lies.

Perfectionism is a mode of life we enter into in an attempt to make ourselves acceptable to establish value and personal worth. It is the insidious dance that puts us on the treadmill of slavery to an identity we're not sure of but hope everyone buys into. This dance is insidious because it turns to tyranny, and over time the real us is lost.

I often meet with people who are bound and determined to know what happened to them and why, feeling that if they simply understood all the circumstances and motivations of everyone involved in the destructive event(s) of their lives they could finally resolve the issue. The Bible tells us that Jesus said, "*You shall know the truth, and the truth shall make you free*" (John 14:6). Unfortunately, because of our performance, we have misinterpreted that verse according to the way of this world; we have thought that "knowing the truth" means gaining more knowledge about the reasons behind the wounds and the circumstances of life that keep us boxed in.

The reality is that knowledge about what happened and understanding the motivations of those who caused it never does give us freedom. It just gives us more information. So we doubt what Jesus told us. Information is not necessarily the truth. The fact is truth is a person. It is knowing the person (Jesus) that sets us free.

Understanding performance or perfectionism won't do anything for you, other than possibly making you more frustrated with yourself and the decisions you made as a kid. Jesus said a few significant things regarding this subject: "*I am the way, the truth and the life*" (John 14:6); "*. . . the words I speak to you, they are spirit and they are life*" (John 6:63). Truth is indeed a person, and it is the interaction with that person that allows His words to pierce to the heart of the matter and make permanent changes in us. I can tell you the truth all day long, but it will never make the impact or the changes necessary to make you free.

The Foundation

Perfectionism is ultimately a spiritual problem and must initially be dealt with from that perspective. Without this perspective, the process would become nothing more than an exercise in attempted behavior modification, and would only prove to be marginally successful.

Perfectionism is not "a" spirit—but it may well be the results of several spirits, depending upon your situation. Realistically, it has as much to do with iniquitous belief structures as demonic influence. These are the invisible iniquitous structures built in your family, which were reinforced by your parents and grandparents.

It is exceptionally sad to see how many people have been raised in, and continue to be mired in, "the system" of this world and have absolutely no clue what they are mired in. They are totally miserable . . . and yet they have no idea why. To escape the pressure and the grind of it would seem to send them headlong into a place they've tried to escape all their lives.

I initially started making notes on this issue in 1994 because of the number of individuals I was ministering to who were struggling with intimacy with God, as well as intimacy with their spouses. I have been at it off and on since then – still trying to make it "perfect." A trip to Hawaii in 2010 (to work with a group that ministered to local women being pulled from the sex trade) highlighted this issue with intimacy in a manner that brought some urgency to it. And, in the process of dealing with the spiritual effects of performance and perfectionism, I have even come face-to-face with my own performance issues.

We have an enemy, and satan and his minions are afraid of you. This is because; a) you were created in the image of God (and that makes him mad enough, if that were the end of it); b) you were created with a unique purpose, to express a flavor of the glory of God that He designed into you; c) there were specific things He created for you to do that demonstrate to satan and people on the earth that God is great and satan is an idiot; and d) fully experiencing "b" and "c" brings personal fulfillment, or the life Jesus spoke of in John 10:10.

In order to keep "b" and "d" from happening, satan has created a series of plans to keep you from fully actualizing the real you in the earth. To do that satan introduces us to what Jesus loosely described as "tribulation" in John16:33. These are spiritual, emotional, and physical wounds: accidents, injuries, traumas, rejection, abandonment, betrayal, deaths, divorces, diseases, disasters, and basically anything bad that strikes at the very core of who you are. In other words, God is good and satan is bad. The source of these "tribulations" are the various demonic entities whose functions are to attack you and then bring one of three lies for you to grab onto.

The lies are always:
    (a) About you: "I'm not good enough. I'm not strong enough, smart enough, loveable, quick enough, and bad things will always happen to me. I'll never make it, I'll never be successful, and I can't paint, dance, sing, read, do math, speak in public, or whatever."

(b) About others at the center of the incident: "They don't love me. No one will protect me. They don't care about me. No one loves me. Everyone will always leave me, etc."

(c) About God: "He doesn't like me, isn't there for me, is distant and unapproachable, isn't interested in me, and I can never live up to His standard, etc."

These lies are meant to play upon all the negative events in your life so that when you look back over them you'll say, "*See there, blah-blah-blah is true because all these experiences prove it.*" Your experiences may not declare *the* truth, but they are *your* truth. It is your truth that determines how you live, relate to others, take chances, and make choices.

The weight of all the negative stuff we experience in life is calculated by the enemy to get you to become somebody else—someone that you believe might be more popular, more likeable, more acceptable, more loveable, less rejectable, etc. We've all done it on some level and have tacitly agreed with satan without the slightest understanding that in doing so we forfeit a chunk of our purpose here on the earth and block ourselves from experiencing all of life at it was supposed to.

He wins. You lose. But you don't have to become demon possessed to miss your destiny; you just have to react wrongly to the events of life. One of satan's favorite ploys is to adopt perfectionism. It has worked so well that he's convinced whole societies across the breadth of the earth that it's the way to go. So we see it everywhere, everyday. We think it's normal because in this temporal realm it is normal.

You don't have to live that way. In fact, you shouldn't!

The Foundation: The Ultimate Origins

Our Western culture is steeped in performance and perfectionism. At its heart are the American ideals of independence and self reliance. This ideal has been romanticized for a 100 years by the motion picture industry featuring the likes of Errol Flynn, the romantic swashbuckler; John Wayne, the hardened cowboy with definitive boundaries, a medium-short temper, and a propensity to break your face with his fist if crossed; the loveable loser of Humphrey Bogart as Rick in Casablanca; or Harrison Ford in the role of Han Solo, the drifter who always took up the side of the disadvantaged underdog.

These characters portray the Western idealism that real men are loners who are only in need of a good horse and a reliable gun, who have no responsibility other than to themselves, and whose only loves were a good stiff drink now and then and the freedom to come and go as they pleased. It always works in the movies, but in reality perfectionism and performance are the absolute antithesis of that ideal.

Worse still is the Christianized version that believes that all we need is Jesus. There is truth in that view, but just enough to get you into trouble.

Where did it all begin?

I believe that it began long before recorded history.

The Bible gives us numerous clues as to the origins and appears to lay out the story of the ultimate conflict between good and evil, unfortunately we're at the center of the story. We are told that after God created an environment for man to thrive in He created a man in His image to inhabit that created place: *"And God created man in his own image, in the image of God created he him; male and female created he them"*; *"And God saw everything that he had made, and, behold, it was very good"* (Genesis 1:27, 31).

In John 4:24, we read, *"God is a Spirit: and they that worship him must worship in spirit and truth."* So God created spirit beings (you and me) just like himself; ergo by Scriptural definition we are primarily spirit beings. Therefore, we must begin to relate to all things created (including one another) from that singular perspective. Most of the misery of man, to the devil's delight, is directly due to the fact that we sincerely believe that events in the spirit are totally separate (if discernible at all) from the natural and thus completely ignorable when compared to everything else that we experience in the earth.

The concept of humans as predominately spirit beings is also stated in 1 Thessalonians 5:23, *"And the God of peace himself sanctify you wholly; and may your spirit and soul and body be preserved entire, without blame at the coming of our Lord Jesus Christ."* Now, the key words here are *"spirit and soul and body."* We can parse ourselves for the purpose of examination and definition, but, in point of fact, we cannot divide ourselves functionally. Were I to walk up and kick you in the shins your spirit would be plenty mad at me. Or if I were to betray our friendship, both your spirit and soul would be wounded. And if the wound (betrayal) were significant enough to you, and you refused to forgive me, in time your body would begin to show the effect of it. Such is the nature of our makeup. The only way to stop the damage is the judicious application of other spiritual principles such as forgiveness, canceling judgments, vows, etc.

The problem with our human view is that, although we may acknowledge the presence of our human spirit as being part of our human makeup we pay it no heed because the overwhelming nature of our existence is predominately tactile. We may be emotionally stirred by a great painting, significantly moved by a wonderful piece of music, and we may feel totally at peace when in the company of good friends following a great meal and particularly flavorful glass of wine, but we write it off to being exclusively the responses of the soul.

There is a principle of Scripture interpretation called "The Principle of First Mentioned" that applies. It declares that whenever there is a list of things provided to us in the Bible the first item in the list is the most important relative to those that follow, and the last item in the list is the least important relative to the other items mentioned in the list.

Therefore, 1 Thessalonians 5:23 declares to us the Godly order in which we are to live. Our human spirit is in submission to the Holy Spirit (see Galatians 6:18; Philippians 4:23; 2 Timothy 4:22). In turn, it rules over our soul, and our soul (defined as mind, will, and emotions) then rules over our body. When things get out of order within us, emotionally or physically, it is because either the soul or the body is making the decisions in life. When my body gets uncomfortable because I have eaten too much and exercised too little, it tells my soul that we're going to the mall for a graduation ceremony to the next larger pant size. My spirit then gets dragged to the mall. It's all out of order. Effectively, we live as savages being more concerned with immediate comfort than being engaged with the broad range of complex issues that make up 'quality of life.'

I want to lob one more bomb into your doctrinal nest before we move on to the story at hand. In Jeremiah 1:5, there is another interesting statement; in my personally paraphrased version Jeremiah says, *"The Lord told me that before He formed me in my mother's womb, He had a relationship with me, and during that time He decided that He would set me apart for a specific task as a prophet to the nations."*

According to my reading of this passage, there was apparently a period between which we were created as spirit beings and our assignment to the earth, after which we acquired a body. The word that is translated from the Hebrew in most Bibles and rendered as "knew" is the Hebrew word *Yada*. It is the same word used in Genesis when Adam "knew" Eve, and she conceived a son. It is also the same word used when Abraham "knew" Sarah and she became pregnant.

The thought being conveyed here through the use of that specific word is that there was some significant intimate relational interaction between us (as spirits) and God (as Spirit), in which we beheld Him, felt His love, and experienced his glory among other things. During this period, it is my belief that God determined and instilled (or installed) in us who we were to be (identity) along with our purpose, or the reason why we were to come to the earth. According to Ephesians 2:10, *"For we are his workmanship, created in Christ Jesus unto good works, which God hath before ordained that we should walk in them."* In other words, there were good works determined for us to accomplish before the foundation of the world. And it is my suspicion that God installed in us everything we would need to accomplish those works, including the desires of our heart that would draw us to them. Psalm 37:4 says, *"Delight thyself also in the LORD; and he shall give thee the desires of thine heart."* My understanding of this verse is that the desires are already in you. We simply need Him to help us discover them, as well as in the process of the realization of them.

The point is that our true identity and purpose was pre-installed before we made our appearance here on the earth in the womb of our mother. Consequently, at least initially, we may have even had a pretty good idea why we were here and what we were to engage in because it tended to line up with our innate heart-felt desires.

It was also during this time that God installed in us everything we would need to fulfill that purpose: intellect, personality, temperament, gifts, skills, abilities, talents, spiritual gifts, curiosity, drive, sense of humor, redemptive gift(s), sensitivity, etc. (2Peter 1:3 *According as his divine power hath given unto us all things that pertain unto life and godliness,*(KJV)) Nothing was left out that was required in order to see that we could do everything He planned for us to accomplish before the foundation of the world.

The problem is that we have an enemy who was probably present when all this creation and installation process was in full swing. He took note of who got what and why. In fact, he probably applauded God's handiwork and creativity as he witnessed each of us being specially crafted.

Later, there was a war in Heaven; lucifer lost, and he and his whole rebellious crew were booted out of Heaven: *"And he (Jesus) said unto them, I beheld satan as lightning fall from heaven"* (Luke 10:18, Revelation 12:7-9, Isaiah 14:12-19, 2 Peter 2:4, Ezekiel 28:14-15). Unfortunately, his high impact destination was the earth where he became known: *"Wherein in time past ye walked according to the course of this world, according to the prince of the power of the air, the spirit that now worketh in the children of disobedience."* (Ephesians 2:2). The war continues to this day.

This is why I feel that we are born with an internal cry to connect with God. However, because we are in the domain of the "prince of the power of the air" who caused a veil to close between us and the one who sent us, all those communication means were cut off. Because when we entered the womb of our mother we didn't have a developed brain in which to store them, all the memories of those bygone days evaporated. Just a hint of them remained. We were also cut off from the all consuming love of God, and we try as hard as we can to replace it with whatever we can grab hold of. We come into this world expecting to be recognized, appreciated, and valued just like it was in our previous abode, but we're in a different time zone, we have a foreign zip code, and can't seem to make it happen.

Contributing to our initial feeling of disconnectedness is the fact that most women don't immediately recognize they are pregnant, some for two months or more. All that time we are hanging out in the womb expecting a party to be thrown in our honor. For many it never happens at all. Despite the fact that we have but a small portion of a developed brain to help us figure this out, our human spirit is alive, well, and ready to function—taking it all in while in a reasonably safe but definitely foreign environment.

This is why scientists have been telling us for the past fifteen to twenty years that there is all manner of unexplained activity exhibited by a fetus in the womb; it cries, it responds to the mother's emotion, and it responds to external stimuli like music, prayer, and the soothing sound of the mother's voice. But it also responds to lack of acceptance, rejection, violence to the mother intended for the child, threats of abortion, harmful chemicals, a hostile external environment, and curse words directed toward it.

And this is just the start. Jesus said in John 16:33 that we would have tribulation, but we just don't expect it to start so early.

Back in 2003 or 2004, my wife and I had opportunity to minister to a woman in her 50's who was preparing to make her dreaded annual pilgrimage to see her aging mother in another state. She dreaded the trip every year because as she said, *"It's a week of continuous agitation. When I get back I'm totally frazzled and worn out! I hate it! And I don't want to go, but I have to."*

There is a ministry technique pioneered by John and Paula Sanford that walks a person through each month of their gestation period and finally through the birthing process to discover what they were feeling/sensing. Its goal is to determine what the person heard, what the person responded to, and what, if any, decisions may have made about the person during that time.

When we got to month seven, the woman said, *"There! She [her mother] said it! She said, 'I'll never love this one like the first.'"* If you have had multiple children, you may recall being faced with the thought, "How can I possibly love the second child as much as I love my first?" It is not a judgment or even a declaration. It is simply a recognition of the wonder of being totally overwhelmed with love.

This woman heard something different. We went back to that point and asked her to recall it again. She did, and this time she heard it correctly, *"I wonder if I'll ever love this one like the first?"* And it was instantly connected with the experiences she had also had with the birth of her children. We walked her through a prayer renouncing her previous belief, forgiving her mother and herself and making a choice to bond with her mother. She left to see her mother the next day.

When we saw her two weeks later, she reported that she had an absolutely amazing trip. She had a wonderful time with her mother and was planning to go back in a couple of months. Then she said, *"You know, my mother told me that from the time I was born I would never let her hold me or cuddle me. I wouldn't sit on her lap or even let her console me if got hurt. Imagine that!"*

The point of this story is that even while we're in the womb, while our brain is still in development, the enemy is working hard trying to get us to improperly react to misinformation in an attempt to crush us.

"Every parent is at some time the father (mother) of the unreturned prodigal, with nothing to do but keep his house open to hope." - John Ciardi

The Foundation: Phase Two

God designed the family specifically to allow our foundational relationships to introduce us to the characteristics of the Godhead: our earthly mother represents the character and function of the Holy Spirit; our earthly Father represents the character, support, and ability of our heavenly Father; and our siblings and extended family members represent the person of Jesus. If our foundational relationships are solid, nurturing, and supportive, when it comes time to be introduced to the Godhead, we experience few problems connecting with each of them. However, if these foundational relationships were deficient when we needed them, the introduction doesn't fare as well.

FATHER	Identity Protection Provision Affection/Kindness Personal Interest Presence Reliability Affirmation Empowerment Authority	**FATHER GOD**
SIBLINGS/ FRIENDS	Companionship Communication	**JESUS**

MOTHER	Trust Comfort Nurture Teacher Unconditional Love	HOLY SPIRIT

The Table above simply denotes those early foundational things which our earthly parental and sibling relationships are supposed to build into us. Later in life, these investments help us get easily introduced to the members of the Godhead. Fortunately, the Lord can do this for us if our parents were unable to.

Childhood Development: Some Interesting Facts

Our brains are divided into multiple parts, which accomplish multiple functions. The principle division is right and left, called hemispheres. The right side controls all left-side body functions. The left side controls all right-side body functions. Intellectually, the left side handles spoken language, number skills, strategy and control, written language, reading, logic and reasoning skills. The right handles the more creative elements: passion, artistic and musical awareness, experience based learning, intuition, and imagination, likely even all communication with our human spirit and the Holy Spirit.

The human brain is an amazing facet of our creation, and we need it to function at peak efficiency in order to maintain physical and emotional health. The effects of trauma primarily impacts six areas of the brain with fairly startling results. The first area is the de-synchronization of the two hemispheres of the brain. This tends to ensure that the left hemisphere becomes dominant and the more intuitive emotionally connected side becomes secondary. This is indicative of a life lived out of the head rather than the heart—one of the major byproducts of perfectionism.

The other areas are: the amygdala, the gate for event storage in memory, as well as the originator of the fight or flight signal; the thalamus, the attachment center (along with the regulation of consciousness, sleep, and alertness); the hippocampus, which is the regulator of memory function and plays important roles in the consolidation of information from short-term memory to long-term memory and spatial navigation; the cingulate cortex, which is involved with emotion formation and processing, learning, and memory; and the right pre-frontal cortex, the joy center and seat of focused attention (planning complex cognitive behavior, personality expression, decision making, and moderating social behavior).

When significant trauma occurs, brain activity begins to migrate from the front of the brain to the back of the brain. The front of the brain has much of the information that determines your identity, i.e. how you act and relate to the world. It is it also home to the glands which regulate joy and quiet, compassion, and sorrow. The back of the brain manages everything needed for survival: hunger, temperature regulation, sleep, hygiene, sex drive, just the basics. The left rear portion of the brain doesn't do joy, or relationships (including God) or creativity on any significant level.

Another result of trauma is the brain activity tends to be maximized in the left hemisphere of the brain, which is the side that handles mathematics, logic, etc. It's primarily knowledge based and is only good at solving problems where logic and knowledge are particularly useful. The right side, which deals more with experienced based understanding, processing of emotional responses, relational issues, and probably even hearing God, is forced to take a back seat.

Because activity in the right pre-frontal cortex tends to diminish over time, it becomes more and more difficult to return to a place of joy or peace after something upsetting occurs. That simply makes it easier for disappointment to lead to depression and to suicidal thoughts, which if unchecked can lead to actualization of the thoughts. For most highly traumatized individuals (as well as perfectionists), drug use becomes an issue in an attempt to self-medicate to stimulate joy and return to a place that feels alive, even if it's short lived.

Childhood Development: From Birth to Age Two

When a child is born, he or she is normally nurtured and cared for by a parent that takes care of all their needs. They are fed when hungry, burped when needed, changed when wet, bathed when dirty, held when crying, talked to in strange tones in spite of the fact that they have no idea what is being communicated, and generally given great amounts of attention, invited or not. The act of breast or bottle feeding augments the process of spirit-to-spirit bonding and loving nurturing of the child by the mother because the child is held close to the parent and frequent, if not continuous, eye contact is held. The child usually has 100 percent of the caregiver's attention during the initial months of life. The embrace is warm, secure, comforting, loving, trustworthy, nurturing, relaxing, and enfolds the child in an environment that helps to ensure that all forms of his or her development are positive. According to Psalm 22:9, *"But you are he that took me out of the womb; You did make me (caused me to learn) trust when I was upon my mother's breasts."*

It is during the first year of life that the child gains trust—or fails to. Paula Sanford notes, "Basic trust is that capacity to hold the heart open, to risk in sustained heart-to-heart involvement with imperfect people. Basic trust is the inner strength and resilience necessary to human relationships, the capacity to remain vulnerable to people who cannot always be believed" (*Transformation of the Inner Man*, 168).

A child's early development is pretty well structured with respect to what needs to be built in, and by whom, in order for the child to be healthy and well adjusted. The first person up to bat, for obvious reasons, is mom. She is the primary person giving input into a child between birth and age two. Between birth and two, the mother instills in the child a sense that they are important, they are safe, they are cared for, and, by her actions begins to demonstrate unconditional love and the idea that parents can be trusted. This all falls under the convenient heading of nurturing. It is this safe, loving environment that allows for the blossoming of all creative gifting within the child. It continues on at some level until about the age of six when basic relational skills become a major thrust, when mom adds an additional dimension of instilling understanding and knowledge (see Proverbs 1:8).

Proverbs 29:15 notes, *"The rod and reproof give wisdom; But a child left to himself bringeth his mother to shame."*

Along with the nurture and comfort comes the introduction of the rudiments of personal discipline, primarily imparted via voice tone, voice volume, facial expression, and body language, and helped along perhaps with an occasional swat on the butt as they grow older. This input continues at a fairly high level through roughly age six when the child's cognitive reasoning ability begins to come online so that cause-and-effect becomes a significant part of decision making.

It is natural that a child wants to please his or her parents. It is part of love. We have mistakenly believed that the ability to please our parents is the mechanism wherein self worth is established. But it is actually the giving of love unconditionally by a parent that produces self worth in the child. By believing that self worth is built through pleasing parents, it makes it all about the child and their own ability and responsibility to provide for themselves. It's certainly not about their ability where establishing self worth is concerned because the potential for failure is quite large. That's the reason God gave us parents in the first place. As predominately emotionally driven little children, it is easy to become convinced that it's all about us, for there is no other frame of reference. And, in the absence of cognitive reasoning skills, we don't want another frame of reference. Through the absence of an abundance of unconditional love, we are made certain that it's all about us because of our emotional pain. So we must pursue what we need for ourselves, doing so on our own terms.

When the parental relationship is dysfunctional, the parent is unable to convey to the child that he or she is loved and accepted just the way they are. Instead, the child believes he or she has to earn love, acceptance, and favor by things they do, if indeed they are able to receive it at all. Then the love, acceptance, attention, and favor of the parent becomes a tool for control and manipulation. What should be free must now be earned. When love must be earned, the child begins to establish a series of standards by which performance for acceptance is measured and by which appreciation is felt emotionally. Those standards are never set at a level of mediocre.

A Father's Influence

When a child approaches two years of age, the drive to establish personal identity emerges. This is when a parent begins to hear a constant chorus of, "I do it myself," coupled with "look at me." With this emergence, the presence and influence of the birth father comes to the fore. It is the father's responsibility to provide identity to the child.

Identity is defined as the characteristics of an individual that are the same throughout the life time of the individual, such that although we grow and adapt to different life circumstances, we essentially remain the same person and can be identified from the characteristics of that sameness. We may from time to time be event synchronic, but over time the principle elements of our personality, character and world view remain much the same.

This is accomplished in multiple ways, but the principle mechanism is spending time with the child passing on to them those things which we have come to value and have proven helpful in living. These things can be good or bad because we find that some things are more easily 'caught' rather than taught. Often the things that are 'caught' are not what we intended to convey. To every child, their mother and father are the two most influential and important things in life. It is through consistent interaction with the child that he or she learns that they are someone important and therefore have innate value as a human being. It is simply built through positive interaction.

One aspect of a father's ability to impart identity at a young age is seen in the manner a father holds a child. Mothers tend to hold their child chest to chest, the position of comfort. More often than not, however, you'll find a father carrying his child so that he or she faces outward, rather like a football. This is a very important position because it anchors the child securely to the father, but it is also the father's subconscious means of introducing the child to the world—first to extended family, then friends and work associates, and then to the world at large. This position also tells the child that he or she is in a place of protection as they gain social and familial awareness.

The fact that a responsible father works and thus takes care of his family's financial needs also reinforces security in a child. But working and providing for the needs of the family is not a substitute for time spent with a child. As noted in the first chapter, bad short-term decisions repeatedly made over time also make for really bad long-term consequences for the child.

If you have ever had children, you will easily recall the times you returned home to see your child playing in the yard, or on the floor in the living room, and heard him or her say, "Look at me. Look at me!" This is the normal response for a child when seeing a parent after an absence because the parents are the ones to establish value in the child. They are the most important persons in the world to the child. It's simply a signal from the child that he or she needs some attention. The combination of that signal, coupled with the striving for independent behavior ("I can do it myself!") should tell a parent to ratchet up the time spent with the child.

If either or both of these foundational relationships are dysfunctional, relationally non-functional, or the parents are physically and/or emotionally unavailable to the child, there will be an identity (value) deficit the child will try to fill it for him or herself. Over time there will be an urgency added to these attempts to establish a sense of personal value. This is when and where the enemy often gains a foothold.

The ploy is always the same: the child needs to establish value for themselves, so a great strategy is to do something new which is praiseworthy. Invariably, when a child does something new it is both noticed and praised (unless of course it's either dangerous or destructive, in which case it's certainly noticed and immediately followed by something other than praise.) Either way, the child takes note of the response and repeats the procedure for additional results. If it again results in praise and adulation, the child is hooked. And the seeds of performance are sewn.

The unforeseen problem is that "new" wears off quickly, and something else must be substituted to get a similar positive response. As the child tries harder to get attention, performance escalates to perfectionism: "I must do things perfectly in order to receive praise." And the belief system is established, which ultimately becomes: "I have value if I do things well; therefore, I must avoid failure at all costs."

Other elements that the father is to instill in the child are:

- **Protection**: physical security or a sense of being protected. Obviously, any sort of abuse destroys it, unfortunately for a life time.

- **Provision**: meeting the physical needs of the family brings a measure of security, even if it's on a meager level when times are tough. It is also one way of teaching (modeling) work ethic. In my case, when the absenteeism and emotional unavailability of my father left me with a poor model of fatherhood, I was at least presented with what my father apparently valued, namely hard work.
- **Affection/Kindness**: appropriate interaction complete with demonstrations of affection always declares to a child that they are loved and acceptable, and that this is the manner in which it is demonstrated to others. Frequent and appropriate public demonstrations of affection between spouses also makes provision for a sense of security for the child, as well as declaring that this is the manner in which love is expressed.
- **Personal Interest**: time spent with a child must include activities that they enjoy, not simply taking them with you to participate in what you enjoy, although that is certainly part of the process. This signals that the parent understands who they are and that what they like is important and therefore has intrinsic value. This could be defined as "quality time," but it is not a substitute for quantity. It determines the child's make-or-break perception of parental availability and connectedness.
- **Presence**: just being around as well as physically and emotionally available to them because being approachable is fundamentally important to development. This must be a

mixture of quantity and quality time. Who will they emulate if their father is not around? Presence must also include interaction with the child for this is the principle means by which values are inculcated.
- **Reliability**: keeping promises is a big deal both to a child as well as everyone else in the family setting. It defines a significant element of true character. Will you say what you mean and mean what you say?
- **Affirmation**: praise for actions of character as well as other accomplishments, including the necessity of expressions of appreciation for participation in various family responsibilities. This is one of the major contributors to training as well as establishing personal value.
- **Empowerment**: allowing children to tackle things on their own (with appropriate supervision) is a significant key to providing children with avenues for building self-confidence and forges a pathway for the pursuit of personal dreams and vision for their lives.
- **Authority**: respect for authority begins and ends with a father. It must be pursued diligently through the teenage years. Improper or heavy-handed demonstrations of it breed rebellion and anarchy in the heart of a child. But with authority comes responsibility. Failure to nurture it and to chastise appropriately determines whether authority is accepted or rejected.

Obviously, this is not an exhaustive list, and on the surface it would seem to minimize the scope of input of the mother on a child's life. That is certainly not the intention or the truth. However, the lack of true fathers and their active participation in the lives of their children has had a major negative effect on American culture.

What we have experienced socially in the last ten years is enough to convict us. Despite all the public angst over the murder of twenty children in their school in Newtown, CT by a mentally deranged son of a teacher, which will change the face of 2nd Amendment rights across the nation, Chicago has had twenty-five times as many gang-related murders annually for the past nine years straight and no one seems to be upset about it. This is in spite of the fact that mass murders are statistically at exactly the same level they have been for the last 20 years.

The number of abortions in America is grinding on and has produced a massive industry that consumed in excess of $2.37 billion in public funds in 2010 (Guttmacher Institute, http://www.guttmacher.org/pubs/Public-Funding-FP-2010.pdf).

The percentage of first births to women living with a male partners (as opposed to being married) jumped from only 12 percent in 2002 to 22 percent between 2009 and 2010—an 83 percent increase. (The National Center for Health Statistics, 2010.). Whoopie! That is certainly good news, but it means that over three-quarters of the children born in 2010 are without the single most critical element in the determination of whether they become productive, mentally and emotionally healthy individuals. Sexual freedom isn't free; someone always pays the price.

The sexualization of the American entertainment industry (TV, movies, magazines, and the internet) regularly produces public images that would have been strictly taboo twenty years ago. Hollywood has earned the USA the 21st Century's equivalent morality title of the 50's, The Ugly American.

Don't get me wrong. I am for the church. It just can't seem to recognize that it has a problem. Fifteen years ago George Barna, the noted Christian researcher, stated as a result of his research that the fastest growing segment of the church in America was, "The Formerly Churched." If you are not producing fathers and mothers, or making a solid place for the few that naturally emerge, you are not getting anything done in the kingdom.

The failure of true fathers and mothers to be raised up in the American church has caused the church to institutionalize those roles to the detriment of our society and the church. The words 'community' and 'family' are used on a wholesale basis in an attempt to describe its potential inclusiveness and ability to meet the needs of its adherents. But if two to three hours per week were all a child could get from a family he/she would be better off in foster care.

When "Christians" consistently vote their wallets instead of their values, we have to say that the church has failed miserably to impart its values to its constituents, not to mention a lost and dying world. When hierarchical titles or roles, rather than mothers and father, are the determining factor in who has to deal with an issue, the authority to speak into that situation or ideology is only as strong as the individual's commitment to the institution. You can resign from an institution, but you can't resign from a family. The church's failure to model one over the other is killing our nation – and it's on the church's watch!

It seems that we know the price of everything these days – but the value of nothing.

Understanding Birth Order

I don't know what the statistics are, but it is my guess that roughly 70 percent of first-born children would consider themselves to be perfectionists. Younger siblings may catch it too if either or both parents are afflicted with it. The last born generally has a much lower percentage of the occurrence, with an exception if the child is the first born male or female behind a string of opposite sex siblings. In these situations, although the child may be down the ladder in the birth order, he or she may adopt many first-born characteristics.

I remember working with a middle-aged woman who was having serious relational difficulty with her husband. He had just ended an affair, and they were on their way to divorce court. When I began praying about the situation, all God said was, *"Classic Case."* As I waited further, nothing more came. Later, as I began relating to her what to expect in the ministry session, the question came to my mind, "Where are you in the birth order?" She was the first of three children. That was all she needed to say. I gave her a list of her symptoms; it was like reading from a book, and I was able to nail every issue she was dealing with. In essence, it was just as advertised, a *"Classic Case."*

First-born children are in a sense the "experimental children." Since parenthood doesn't come with a manual, the parents of first-born children are often young and inexperienced in many other life skills. Parents pick and choose what to do in a reactionary mode from anything they have ever heard anyone say, and perhaps from convoluted logic if there is no other input. Many first-born children are even raised by children themselves. In our age of two-income families, many children are actually raising themselves. First-born children are usually born to very young parents whose full range of problem solving skills have not yet been developed. They often have their own insecurity issues and have not developed either the patience or self-control necessary to properly raise children.

We have some good friends who's son and daughter-in-law are justifiably proud of their three-year old first born daughter. She is 'very responsible.' They are totally unaware of the issues she will have later as they raise their 'little adult' depending upon her at this age to pack her own bag for a week-long trip, without supervision.

Another thing that typically raises the chance of having to deal with perfectionism is if there are three or more years between children. The older sibling, as well as the younger will tend to have a number of first-born traits, and it's pretty much assured if they are of opposite sex. Dr. Kevin Leman's *The New Birth Order Book* sheds some important light on the effects of birth order on the characteristics of various birth orders. In our fractured-family world, we are all too familiar with children that are products of divorced parents who remarry and sometimes then have children of their own. Many times there is a significant age gap between the products of these relationships, which produces multiple children with first-born characteristics among those who are below age five.

Leman's birth order characteristics are generalizations of course. They can be modified by parenting skills (or lack thereof), redemptive gifts of the child, the home environment, socio-economic situations and several other factors. But they are a great place to begin.

Leman gives the following listing of general potential personality traits for each of the possible birth orders:

Characteristics of the **First Born** can generally be described as follows: perfectionist, reliable, conscientious, list-maker, well organized, hard-driving, natural leader, critical, serious, scholarly, doesn't like surprises, loves computers.

Characteristics of an **Only Child** can generally be described as follows: little adult by age seven, very thorough, deliberate, high achiever, self-motivated, fearful, uses "very" and "extremely" a lot, can't bear to fail, very high expectations for self.

Characteristics of the **Middle Born** can generally be described as follows: mediator, compromising, diplomatic, avoids conflict, independent, loyal to peers, many friends, a maverick, secretive, unspoiled.

Characteristics of the **Last Born** can generally be described as follows: manipulative, charming, blames others, attention-seeker, tenacious, people person, natural salesperson, precocious, engaging, affectionate, loves surprises.

Birth Order has been the subject of study since the late 1600's and although birth order is far from an exact science, because there are many things which can skew it such as the number of years between children, it is quite helpful in understanding how people relate to their circumstances and what parental issues they are likely to be dealing with. When you have some tangible clues of this nature, the Holy Spirit can use your knowledge of human behavior to help point the way to the root issue that is causing all the pain and turmoil.

I have had occasions to minister to a number of first-born children of abusive fathers and have found that Leman's birth order trait descriptions are quite helpful in determining why they suffer as they do. Because they display an inordinate desire to please, as demonstrated in their perfectionist tendencies, if their father was quite critical and/or abusive, they may have adopted what Leman calls the "Discouraged Perfectionist Syndrome." This drives them to a decision point: do I just give up and grow angry, or do I stubbornly go on and attempt to only please myself? (Either decision produces angry people.) The difficulty with either approach is that the first born can no more deny his or her perfectionist tendencies than they can fly.

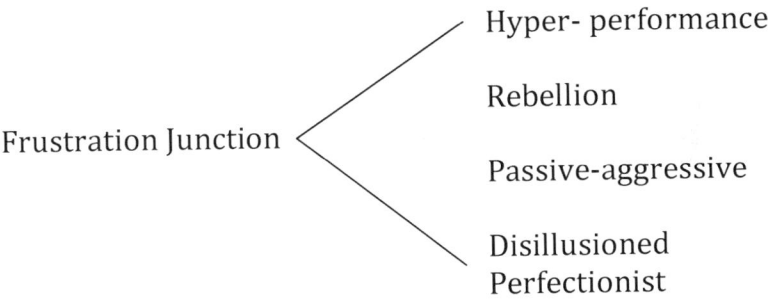

Frustration Junction
- Hyper- performance
- Rebellion
- Passive-aggressive
- Disillusioned Perfectionist

The result is that perfectionists easily transfer their allegiance from their fathers to others, bosses, authorities, etc., who are also unfortunately human and fail them just as their own natural father did. So they have all manner of authority issues. Their personal standards are sufficiently unachievable, no matter what they produce, and they live in state of perpetual frustration, which contributes to a high level of anger and rebellion.

Now, because natural affection was never received as a child, perfectionists suffer from severe broken hearts. In an attempt to keep out hurt and avoid being wounded further, walls are raised. The paradox is that the very walls used for defense are also the same walls that keep out the love they so desperately desire. Tragically, the wall raised for protection against pain indiscriminately keeps out the very thing needed to survive and flourish.

The bottom line is that no matter how hard they try at love, they will not allow themselves to receive love under any circumstances because their inner truth is, "I really have no value. If I really let you in, you'll get close enough to recognize it and reject me." They usually wind up in sexual sin, numerous affairs, fantasy lives, pornography, etc. because the natural physical expressions of "love" often become confused with the real thing.

As life begins to unfold it become harder and harder for their dreams, aspirations, or hopes to become realized, life seems to adopt a downward spiral. Many adolescents become terminally discouraged with life. In doing so, they adopt a world view that they will always lose—that no one could possibly love them, that everyone is against them, and that nothing good will ever happen. Self esteem totally evaporates, and they retreat within themselves in order to try to find some solace in their desperate existence. Fortunately, the survival instinct is so strong in the vast majority of people that suicide is only a thought, otherwise we would be in jeopardy of losing an entire generation in today's fatherless society.

Certainly not every first-born or only child has this same experience. Because of their drive most will be fairly successful financially and be able to function at a very high level in the business and social environments. Love will eventually strike a blow and they'll pair off and attempt life from a different perspective. It is the intimacy of relationship over an extended period of time where the wheels begin to fall off. That's where real life is found.

When a first born marries a first born, life will be very interesting. If one mate's standards are not able to produce a sufficient amount of personal frustration, the other will come along side and provide what is lacking. The rigidity of the environment they create together will emphasize order, precision, and predictability. There will be little room for spontaneity. The problem with all this is that they are doing it all naturally and don't have any idea it is going on. So not only is there a level of inner healing and potential deliverance required to heal the broken hearts and handle the authority issues, they actually have to renew their minds in order to deliver themselves from being slaves to their natural perfectionist tendencies and learned behavior in order to make real progress.

Without knowing something about birth order and its behavioral characteristics, you will have to allow the Holy Spirit to take you on a long circuitous route to get to the root issue.

If the individual is an only child, they generally have the full dose, just an extra measure of it. If their parents were professional who were strict and absorbed totally in their endeavors, they have a double dose. They not only had to deal with parental issues, they had to deal with God at the same time.

The good news in all this is that the Holy Spirit knows them inside and out and knows exactly how to get to the root of the issue: how to get their attention, how to have you express the root issue to them in a way only they can receive it, how to have you pray, and how to minister healing to them in the most effective manner. So if you will stay close to Him in this process—and it is a process—several He promises the following:

> *"I will not drive them out from before you in one year; lest the land become desolate, and the beast of the field multiply against you. By little and little I will drive them out from before you, until you be increased, and inherit the land."* Exodus 23:29-30

> *"And therefore will the LORD wait, that he may be gracious unto you, and therefore will he be exalted, that he may have mercy upon you: for the LORD is a God of judgment: blessed are all they that wait for him."* Isaiah 30:18

The Lord is most gracious to us in that He doesn't wreck our house of cards all in one fell swoop. He knocks off some here and then a little there so that we don't lose our identity and our minds simultaneously. Then he carefully rebuilds our foundation based upon the Word, so that we both last forever.

My Own Story

I am a first-born child (of a first-born son), displaying the typical array of first-born characteristics previously noted. I was born immediately after the war and my father was busy trying to establish a career for himself to feed his now growing family. My father was the pilot of a C-47 troop carrier during the war. Following the war, the general public had no need—nor desire—to jump out of a perfectly good airplane, but he had a skill he wanted to use. So he bought a small aircraft and hired himself out to oil companies, flying pipeline routes looking for leaks. As you can imagine, this kept him away from home a lot—strike one in the attention receiving ball game.

To complicate matters, shortly after birth, I contracted a malady doctors diagnosed as "pyloric stynosis." This diagnosis describes a condition in which the one-way valve at the entrance to the stomach does not properly function and allows liquid nourishment to immediately leave the stomach rather than trapping it inside. That which was meant to nourish can also enter tiny lungs and cause drowning. So the simple act of burping, which every baby must do to expel the air ingested while feeding, becomes projectile vomiting. To avoid such an event, my mother was told that immediately after feeding I was to be propped up in a crib and not handled. This malady lasted for more than seven months.

> Psalms 22:9 *"But thou art He that took me out the womb: thou didst make me trust when I was upon my mother's breasts."*

Human touch is absolutely necessary for life. If you doubt it, just google "human touch and development" and see what pops up. In one experiment involving babies born prematurely, randomly selected babies were lightly stroked for forty-five minutes per day while the remaining babies were handled sufficient for changing, feeding, and proper daily care. Although all were fed the same amount of calories, after ten days, the touched babies weighed 47 percent heavier than the unstimulated group. Not only were those children bigger, they were happier too. The stroked kids were more active, more alert and more responsive. (See http://www.mindpub.com/art173.htm.)

My father's love of flying was unquenchable, and as a toddler my mother said I always held my breath all the way through takeoff and up until the time we reached altitude, where he would adjust the props from the power climb position. The change in rpms was my signal to breathe again. Nothing like a periodic dose of fear—induced by your father—to make you wonder whose side he's really on. I presume my in utero experience wasn't much different either.

My father's attempts to stay in the flying business never panned out, and in time he wound up grounded, working as a crew chief running a field crew looking for oil to feed the nation's hungry industrial boom. This led to more time away from home, until my mother's protestations at being left alone prompted them to buy a mobile home so they could be together more. Meanwhile, a brother two years my junior had come along to compete for my parents' attention. Four years later, a little sister was thrown in for good measure.

The addition of thirty-two foot trailer made traveling easier, but it added another element of instability to the mix because we were now more mobile than ever. We moved. We moved. And we moved some more—frequently! Between the ages of three and thirteen, my meticulous record keeping mother had documented ninety-seven individual addresses. That's in excess of nine moves a year.

I distinctly remember starting the fourth grade in Houston, TX, moving from there to Opelousas, LA, Lafayette, LA, Baton Rouge, LA, Vicksburg, MS, to two places in the Florida panhandle, back to Opelousas and finally finishing the same school year with the same class I started with back in Houston. During that time, I remember pleading with my mother not to make me go to school in Vicksburg because I knew we would only be there two weeks.

Unfortunately, my mother was unable to help me process all the internal conflict and external stress I was experiencing. It took me years to realize that she was in the same boat that I was. She had no support system for herself either, so probably all she could think of was to get me off to school and out of the house so she could handle the other two.

One of the natural out workings of this nomadic lifestyle wasa the adoption of a Dismissive Attachment Style. Rather than trying to bring closure to issues involving relationships it was much easier to just shut them off. Those that get cut off essentially become dead to you, out of sight-out-of-mind and heart. Consequently, I have had relatively few long-term relationships. None prior to age forty-five or so.

My father started a new career in geophysics when I reached middle school, and his business travel increased. By the time I reached the last years of Junior high school, we had moved permanently to Covington, LA. I saw him only on weekends, and even when he was there, he wasn't there—he either had his head buried in a newspaper or in the Bible preparing to teach a Sunday School class in the Southern Baptist church we attended. During high school, I played four sports all four years; my father attended only one football game during that period. But then I wasn't around the house much either. When I got home from practice it was eat quickly and start homework. Weekends were spent like most active teenagers, trying to recover from the week.

My childhood was not one of a series of rejections but a lifestyle of rejection. My father's physical and emotional unavailability cinched it. As could easily be predicted, I had long since become performance oriented, of that there is no doubt. As a first-born perfectionism was a simple, even natural decision. Somewhere toward the end of middle school, I finally figured out that I would never get my father's attention. I became a "disillusioned perfectionist," and my life took a rather dark inward turn.

Fortunately, because I was raised in church, I had been inoculated with God. After leaving high school, I dabbled with all manner of stuff in a vain attempt to arrest the constant nagging pain I felt. For years I had a mental picture of myself as a toddler, standing in a cloth diaper, alone in some room crying inconsolably. Eight years of marriage provided a respite, but I was ultimately dealt a nearly lethal emotional blow when my wife left me for a tenured professor at the University of Houston where she was studying. The rejection that I had felt the first two-thirds of my life came again with a vengeance. My life was in the toilet, and I felt like there was a heavy hand on the handle.

A therapist in southern California, Dr. Jim Wilder, author of *The Life Model, Living from the Heart That Jesus Gave You* and a major contributor to *Thriving: Recover Your Life*, describes two types of traumatic wounds: Type A, the things a parent does not do for you, and Type B, the things they do to you. From his perspective, Type A father wounds are more damaging to a child because of what is *not* built into, or established in a child through the emotional abandonment—chief among them is personal identity. He also cites them as being the more difficult of the two to recover from.

A Biblical Example

In the book of Matthew, Chapter 19 we find a perfect example of perfectionism and Jesus' diagnosis and prescription for it. You have no doubt heard numerous talks and sermons on the story of the rich young ruler and the destructive power of wealth, and although it is certainly applicable to that point, in actuality, this story really doesn't have much to do with wealth, the striving for it, the accumulation of it, or man's efforts to keep it. Instead it paints a totally different picture, but one that is extremely important because it tells us what God thinks is the most important element in Kingdom life:

> *"Now behold, one came and said to Him, "Good Teacher, what good thing shall I do that I may have eternal life?" So He said to him, "Why do you call Me good? No one is good but One, that is, God. But if you want to enter into life, keep the commandments." He said to Him, "Which ones?" Jesus said, "'You shall not murder,' 'You shall not commit adultery,' 'You shall not steal,' 'You shall not bear false witness,' 'Honor your father and your mother,' and, 'You shall love your neighbor as yourself.'" The young man said to Him, "All these things I have kept from my youth, "What do I still lack?" Jesus said to him, "If you want to be perfect, go, sell what you have and give to the poor, and you will have treasure in heaven; and come, follow Me." But when the young man heard that saying, he went away sorrowful, for he had great possessions. Then Jesus said to His disciples, "Assuredly, I say to you that it is hard for a rich man to enter the kingdom of heaven. And again I say to you, it is easier for a camel to go through the eye of a needle than for a rich man to enter the*

kingdom of God." When His disciples heard it, they were greatly astonished, saying, "Who then can be saved?" (Matthew 19:16-25)

This same story is found from two other perspectives in Mark 10:17-27 and Luke 18:18-27.

The rich young ruler in this passage is obviously a perfectionist because:
    a) he's rich,
    b) he's young,
    c) he's consciously worked on being perfect since he was a child,
    d) he's heavily engaged in checking off everything on his list he considers needful for being declared a success, and
    e) Jesus tips us off in verse 21 with His none-too-discrete *"If you would be perfect."*

He's probably a fellow we would all like. Unless you're in the mafia, or a drug dealer, or into high-end international arms sales. It's very difficult to become wealthy without being likable. After all, even those other guys would exude a certain charm. One has to possess some form of charisma, persuasiveness, and an ability to influence people in order to obtain wealth. Such was this young man. His parents may have given him a monetary head start, but this passage states that he was diligently and thoroughly (even methodically) trying to cover all his bases. He sought to dot all the i's and cross all the "t's so that he might be considered "worthy." In other words, he had apparently sought all his life to establish a sense of value for himself. To do so, he may well have sought out a series of other rabbis, but in this case he sought out "the one" who was making such a stir in the religious countryside—the unconventional guy who "knew stuff" that the ordinary religious guys might not know and the one who was purported to have the "ultimate connection."

The answer Jesus gave to his question ("*What else do I need to check off my list to be qualified, to be valued, to be considered to be a success?*") probably took this young man completely by surprise because he had worked hard to get it all together. He even said that he'd been working on his checklist since he was a child. Proof positive that he thought he'd racked up enough "points" to make it. He certainly didn't get the response he was looking for.

The response of Jesus, "*If you would enter into life . . .*" surely must have caught him off guard. He may have even been shocked. Were you to look around him and compare those in his entourage with his personal achievements, his influence, his business acumen, his wealth, his manners and mode of dress, his personal discipline, surely you would have immediately seen a discernible difference that set him apart from all the others. After all, he had walked this way a long time. He had a reputation, and he had worked hard to cultivate it. The identity he had created for himself was defined by it all, and everything he had accomplished spoke of who he had come to be. Surely you couldn't miss it.

But Jesus was highlighting something that the young man could not see, in fact, something he and every other perfectionist is totally oblivious to. To put a finer point on it, Jesus said that he had to keep some specific commandments straight out of Exodus 20: don't murder, don't commit adultery, don't steal, don't lie about others, honor your father and your mother, and love your neighbor as yourself.

The young gun said, "*Hey, no problem! I've done all that since I was knee high. What's left?*" The difficulty was, the young man had followed all the rules but missed the whole point of the interchange. He had missed the whole point of the Scriptures he had just heard; he had missed the whole point of Jesus' life and the image of the Father he had come to portray. He had missed it all!

You see, perfectionists are driven to be hailed as being worthy of praise for what they do and not for who they are. Who they are has become confused with what they do. In that belief system, personal legitimacy is only achieved by accomplishment and personal competency. Those things never define or establishes personal value. The identity your father was to build into you as a child is never based on what you do, but who you are.

One example is Dennis Rodman. Unfortunately, the ability, the concentration and effort he put into playing basketball never translated to the non-professional side of his life.

Personal validity is never established by the value of what one accomplishes daily, such as making money. The actual importance of what is accomplished on a daily basis is not inconsequential because in order to provide value it must also meet society's goals, i.e. personal wealth, status in the community, and popularity ... and yet it will never satisfy the deepest hunger of the human soul.

The values of the Kingdom of Heaven are not the values of this realm. When Jesus said, "*If you would enter into life . . .,*" He was saying several things.

First, when Jesus said, '*You need to keep all these commandments,*' Jesus wasn't referring to the law at all. He was making a point about relationship, the spirit behind the commandments. Every one of the commandments that He quoted from Exodus 20 pertained solely to how we treat other people. Perfectionism is solely a function of personal performance which cares nothing for those around us. In order to live a "perfected" life, we assume we have to keep a bunch of laws, rules, and regulations governing how performance is measured, which has absolutely nothing to do with relationship. One can keep every commandment down to the letter and yet not have one meaningful life-giving relationship.

On occasion, in order to preserve a relationship we have to say we were wrong, when we were obviously right. A perfectionist can't do that. Does that mean they have to lie? No, it's simply one of the ways we have to prefer someone over ourselves (Philippians 2:4) and lay down our lives in preference for others (John 15:13). But if perfectionism is the ideal, such a stance is highly improbable because saying "I'm sorry" implies that a mistake has been made and perfection will not allow mistakes. One can't live life through the brain trying to figure it all out before acting. Life cannot be calculated. It must be lived through the heart. And that's risky business!

The next thing Jesus was saying was that to live in perfectionism is to live by a host of rules and regulations that we amass personally. These rules and regulations are the things we have gathered along the way that are indispensable to us in determining how to achieve success, avoid failure, and manage the risk of failure. Unfortunately, because we are perfectionists, the laws, rules, and regulations we collect are not just ordinary rules; they establish perfection. We, being human, are not perfect creatures and never will be. The result is a life-long acquaintance with a high level of frustration that we can't even meet our own standards, which becomes the continual background noise of life. The net product is deep-seated anger.

Have you ever thought to yourself, "*If you'll just tell me the rules of the game I'll play?*" That's a big time clue into what we're talking about. Even in the context of a friendly game, with nothing on the line, as a perfectionist you are still trying to assess and accurately measure the risk of failure. In an attempt to disguise it, you rename it something healthier: competitiveness.

The third thing Jesus was saying is that with all the limitations that you unnecessarily put on yourself as a perfectionist, life has become very hard; in fact, you're not living life at all but are merely existing. All the business and activity gives you the illusion of a life simply because you are around people and you have to engage with them on a mostly superficial level to get done what's on your plate. You are engaging their head with your head only. That's not life; it's merely functioning.

The Bible gives us a decidedly different view of what real life is; all the statements have no meaning outside the company of others:

> "*To everything there is a season, and a time to every purpose under the heaven: A time to be born, and a time to die; a time to plant, and a time to pluck up that which is planted; A time to kill, and a time to heal; a time to break down, and a time to build up; A time to weep, and a time to laugh; a time to mourn, and a time*

to dance; A time to cast away stones, and a time to gather stones together; a time to embrace, and a time to refrain from embracing; A time to get, and a time to lose; a time to keep, and a time to cast away; A time to rend, and a time to sew; a time to keep silence, and a time to speak; A time to love, and a time to hate; a time of war, and a time of peace." (Ecclesiastes 3:1-8)

"A man that hath friends must shew himself friendly: and there is a friend that sticketh closer than a brother." (Proverbs 18:24)

"A friend loveth at all times, and a brother is born for adversity." (Proverbs 7:17)

In Matthew 19:17, Jesus states, *"Why do you call me good? There is only one who is good."* In doing so, Jesus was making some significant statements. Jesus was again being true to His mission of properly representing the Father here on the earth. And Jesus was being careful to establish relationship by example through daily giving a faithful report of the one He was related to. He wanted to make sure that the young man knew those who wanted to be rightly related to God should be seeking to be connected to He who is thoroughly good.

When Jesus said *"If you would be perfect . . .,"* He was at once speaking to the ultimate pursuit of the perfectionist and the performance oriented soul: being perfect in the eyes of man, as well as being perfectly fit for the Kingdom of God. The pursuit of perfection, then, is really the pursuit of being accepted, first by those who are most important to us (parents) and then by men, and ultimately by God.

"I have spent hours kicking myself for not fighting past Dad's reserve, for not going into that cave where he lived and rooting him out." - William Plummer, *Wishing My Father Well (2000)*

    I once knew a man who built custom interior stairways. He was a craftsman of great skill and care. Everything he did in that arena was done well. The problem was that his perfectionism required him to go slower than anyone else so he wouldn't make a mistake. He would put in ten to eleven hour days, whereas his fellow craftsmen would only work eight. He only got paid for eight, but he put in many more, not because he was being more productive but simply because it took him so much longer than everyone else due to his perfectionism. His family suffered, and his marriage suffered. But in his mind, as the sole bread winner, he had no choice. He is now divorced and unemployed.

    I have heard innumerable sermons delivered on this passage in the past sixty plus years I have attended church, and almost every pastor, his associate, or a visiting evangelist (or whatever) interprets this passage in accordance with the last four verses as the main subject. Then they invariably latch on to 1 Timothy 6:10: *"For the love of money is the root of all evil: which while some coveted after, they have erred from the faith, and pierced themselves through with many sorrows."* They will even drag in Ecclesiastes 4:8: *"There is one alone, and there is not a second; yea, he hath neither child nor brother: yet is there no end of all his labor; neither is his eye satisfied with riches; neither saith he, For whom do I labor, and bereave my soul of good? This is also vanity, yea, it is a sore travail."*

Consequently, they totally miss the point by making it all about the search for gold as though working for a living were a sin. The reality of life is that we have to earn a living, and if you are engaged in that which the Lord has designed you for, you can expect to be taken care of through the exercise of it. Not only will your God-given gifts and talents make room for you (Proverbs 18:16), but as you express the glory of God through the work of your hands, His favor will be upon you. This is the design of God because the grace of God flows to design not to woundedness.

There is another reality of life we all have to contend with: we not only have an enemy who is against us, but he also uses others as part of his strategy. Consequently, things don't always go as they should. In the engineering field, which is preparatory to the construction that follows, you soon learn the old adage, "Everything takes as long as it takes," which means "it's always going to take longer than you think it should." And so it is with just about every other profession. If the task takes two hours to complete and that's all you have, somebody is going to call with some kind of emergency right in the middle of it. Yes, we try to put up boundaries to protect our time and the time our wives and family deserve, but sometimes stuff takes longer than it should.

Most of the motivation of the church behind pounding on this passage in this manner is that they are blaming the lack of time and attention parishioners give to the programs of their institution because they're "working too hard." For many, it is likely to be a fact, but using the Bible to manipulate the congregants is far from a pure motivation.

The real tragedy here is that even the church doesn't have much of a clue about the fundamental constituent elements that make life worth living. This is never truer than in large cities where living in community is only something the people love to philosophize about but have no concrete idea of how to live out. So it attacks the pursuit of money as the answer to the problem, rather than pursuing it to the root.

If you are a pastor, or even a layperson who's guilty of only telling half the story, you need to apologize for being blinded by the system of the world and completely missing the larger point of the passage, which, by the way, is the real source of the problem.

The Heavy Baggage of Perfectionism

The vast majority of people who suffer from perfectionism may also suffer from a number of other significant peripheral issues, which may or may not have some demonic attachment:

No Childhood Memories: The only childhood memories they have are actually stimulated by or generated as a result of viewing old family photos or have been formed by the narrative memories of relatives. The recounting of stories somehow does not have the same power to recover memories although they may induce some. For most people, no memories equate to possibly having bad memories, or stuffed pain, and consequently the memories are sufficiently suppressed to the extent that they are consciously unavailable. This is often problematic because numerous therapy modalities require the availability of the client's painful memories in order to be effective.

Self-hate: The lack of nurturing from the father/mother generally leaves them with significant self worth issues, and the worst cases have serious health problems. Self-hate is the most common and generally the strongest of the demonically reinforced difficulties. Most have serious back problems, which miraculously go away in concert with the emotional healing and deliverance.

"How true daddy's words were when he said: All children must look after their own upbringing." - Anne Frank

Individuals struggling with this issue have extreme difficulty receiving love because they believe they are not loveable, or perhaps are not worthy of love. Typically, they cannot receive something as simple as a compliment because it finds no place of value to resonate with within them—there was never a landing pad for love or appreciation built in the heart by the parents. It is usually the source of a life-long effort to become validated by what can be accomplished.

The Word declares in Matt 22:39, *"And the second (commandment) is like unto it, You shall love your neighbor as yourself"*; 1 John 4:8, *"He that loves not, knows not God; for God is love"*; and in 1 John 4:20, *"If a man says, I love God, and hates his brother, he is a liar: for he that loves not his brother whom he has seen, how can he love God whom he has not seen?"* The implication here is clear: healthy people should be able to love others, including themselves. It is a relatively simple choice for most people. But for those who are emotionally unhealthy and who have great difficulty opening up to love others, they find themselves to be doubly crippled because they can't receive it either. They also cannot know and love God on an intimate level because that which both gives and receives love (the heart) is wounded and broken. This is often a major frustration for them.

Often times this becomes a difficulty in marriage as it was for the lady who came to me because of her seeming inability to prioritize her life. When one cannot love themselves, they feel that there is nothing in them that is loveable so they cannot receive love. Meanwhile, their spouse is continually pounding at their heart's door trying to get in. First with flowers, then compliments, and then outrageous displays of affection . . . in time, they give up. Not because they don't still love but because, "*Hope deferred makes the heart sick*" (Proverbs 13:12a).

It is indeed unfortunate, but self-hate is a demon and there will be very little relational progress until this thing is excised.

And another thing . . .

There is also another difficulty that is typical, and it is nothing more than religious activity. We feel good about ourselves when we help others. It's the way God made us. Without it there would be no such thing as human charity. But when feeling good about ourselves becomes the motive, rather than a byproduct of our Christian faith and life, our self-sacrifice becomes self-serving; we help others in order to feel better about our own condition. The true motive of our heart is hidden from us such that no one can dare tell us that our "service" is all about us.

According to the Prophet Jeremiah said, "*The heart is deceitful above all things, and desperately wicked; who can know it?*" (Jeremiah 17:9). Obviously, he knew a little about the human heart. So did David; in Psalm 139:23, he states to God, "*Search me, O God, and know my heart: try me, and know my thoughts: And see if there be any wicked way in me, and lead me in the way everlasting.*"

I believe what David was saying to God was this: "Father you know that I have been faithful in the past to deal with every heart issue you brought before me. But I can't deal with what you don't show me. I can't deal with what I don't see. So show me the wicked ways in me, and I'll be honest enough to confess it and deal with it the best I can. Then show me the right way to walk—I'll do that too." Not knowing our own heart, but believing our motives to always be pure, is little more than pride, which is the predecessor of destruction: *"Pride goes before destruction, and a haughty spirit before a fall"* (Proverbs 16:18).

Radical Change as Opportunity for satan

When dealing with someone who is having emotional and spiritual difficulties rooted in childhood, look first to points where radical change occurred in the family. This may be a sudden death, a divorce, the arrival of another child, a parent's loss of a job and the onset of chronic money problems, change of address from the only place they knew as home, a health issue, career change of a parent, a mother going to work, a bad Christmas experience, abuse, trauma, or anything that smacks of significant change from the normal experience. Anything that disturbed what was previously known as a safe, secure sanctuary can be a major key. It can also be a key to unlocking the source and cause of generational curses, as many parallels in family lives can be tracked to a specific time of life or age of the participants.

In particular, look for a radical change that occurred at or before the age of six or seven. It is around this age when children begin to enter into their "cognitive ability," which allows individuals to sort through difficult issues logically. Prior to this time, children operate simply on emotions, and it is the prime time when satan seems to want to attack (in order to pervert understanding of issues). So if significant debilitating lies are apparent, defining the time at which significant change occurred may help pinpoint what the lie was.

A pastor friend of mine and I were ministering to a man in his early 30s whose stated problem was that he was always angry. About every two to three years or so it would come to a boiling point at work, and he would either quit before the bomb went off or get into an argument with his superior and get fired. He had just recently left his job and was tired of the merry-go-round.

As we delved into his past, we found that his relationship with his parents was good as far back as he could remember and it had only gotten better with time. There was no abuse of any description. He had done well in school, both in sports and academics. However, he couldn't seem to stay in a relationship with a woman, because he was much too demanding of himself and always broke them off of his own accord. None of the familiar roots seemed to fit him at all, and we were stumped about where to go next.

As I began to pray, the thought occurred to me to ask him about what was going on in his parent's lives before age eight. He grew up in the house he was born in, so there was no issue there. His mother never worked and had no emotional problems that he was aware of; as well, his brothers and sisters all seemed to be well adjusted and doing well in their marriages and careers. His father was a tenured college professor and was the pillar of the community, as well as the church they attended. Nothing seemed to stick out. But for some reason he seemed to be an angry man. His parents divorced when the youngest child entered college, but he was not aware of why. The only time there seemed to be tension in the house was when his father got passed over for a promotion at the college.

The Holy Spirit then had me ask him what happened at Christmas when you were five or six. Was there anything special or different about it? He paused for a while, trying to recall either of those particular holidays. He began to recall a Christmas morning when he was six. He had gotten a truck for Christmas. He was so excited about it and proud of it, and he wanted to show his father what he had gotten. He kept holding it up in front of him, trying to skirt the newspaper his father was trying to read at the same time. He moved around to his side, held it up again for him to see, and in his exuberance with the new truck, struck his father in the chin with it.

His father instantly blew up! He grabbed the truck from his hands and slung it across the room and told his mother to take care of him. Through great racking sobs, he said he remembered that there was always a slight tension in the air after his father didn't get that promotion that he thought he deserved. (That happened in June the year before.) At the instant of hitting his father with the truck, and seeing his father's anger flare up at him, he thought, "*I am* the reason my father is always angry!" We had finally gotten to the real root of the issue because satan had fed him a lie, trapping him in self-imposed anger for twenty-seven years.

[handwritten margin note: beard incident]

Whenever there is an emotionally charged event in our lives, the enemy is always there to try and help us misinterpret it. If we bite, and we generally do, there are always one of three lies he attempts to sow:

a) one about us: we're not good enough, smart enough, strong enough, or whatever enough, and it's my fault, I'll never get it right, and there's something wrong with me, etc.

    b) one about those involved in the circumstance: they don't love me, they don't care about me, I'm not wanted, I'm always a bother to them, etc.

    c) one about God: He doesn't care about you, He can't help you, He doesn't love you, He distant and otherwise occupied, He's angry and unapproachable, etc.

    Such was the case for our friend noted above.

    The inability to receive a compliment, or any sort of gushy sentimental expressions of love, is founded in self-rejection because we fear that somewhere in the midst of the rejection is the truth: "There really is something wrong with me."

    Being "right" is also a presumed need of a perfectionist because being "wrong" means "I am being rejected," and it means *I* will not be accepted by *you* there's something wrong with me. Their identity has become firmly rooted in what "I believe," which has to be "right" because being "right" means I am right. And if "I'm right" then "I'm *all* right!" Rejection is: "I'm not right," "I'm not all right," "I'm wrong," and "I therefore can't be vulnerable and receive because it means I have to drop walls/guard/defense and that's not safe." Competency (validation) is the only guard a perfectionist has against potential rejection.

Additional Issues . . .

    Self-pity. Chief among the problem-centered, or perhaps more properly self-centered issues to be dealt with is self-pity. It is a form of self-hatred and a close cousin to depression. It is not so much a spirit, although it is reinforced by demonic means, as it is flesh run amuck. If this has becomes a way of life, there is little hope if the individual is not willing (and determined) to break out of it and finally take control of their own mind.

"Blessed is the man who expects nothing, for he shall not be disappointed." - Alexander Pope

Lack of Self Esteem. A function of self-pity, a lack of self esteem is often seen in a dislike for their name, the way they look and/or talk because they cannot accept their personality and generally believe they have limited or no abilities that are useful.

Anger. Anger can have multiple sources, but this is specifically subconscious or unconscious anger that people live with at such a constant background level that they know of no other way to feel. They know they're angry but don't know why. It results in short tempers, over reaction (often violent), or minor offences or irritants and is generally accompanied by a very negative view of life and their lot in it. Anger is also produced by feelings of abandonment, not being valued, various kinds of abuse, the inability to please a parent, or to gain love and acceptance from parents. Whenever we are not fully embraced and nurtured by our parents, the void it leaves in our hearts produces anger.

"It is easier for a father to have a child than for children to have a real father."
- Pope John XXIII

Moreover, anger is also the natural result of perfectionism because there is always a continual level of frustration at work because the extremely high self-imposed standards are not able to be met. And it can also be a result of irresolvable conflicts during childhood, such as a lie presented which says, "I must be a perfect person in order to be a good person." It is met with a reality that says, "I can never be perfect"—ergo, an irresolvable conflict, which the child often attempts to "partially" resolve using intensely faulty logic.

Fear of Failure. This is a biggie because it touches so many areas in life. It is the inability to begin or complete a task or to achieve something deeply desired, or even needed like a better job, because it may end in failure (even if the mark is their own lofty expectations) which results in automatic self-rejection and disapproval. This can be the case long after the parent is deceased and no longer able to pass judgment on any of the adult child's activities.

Fear of Man. The saddest part about falling into fear is that the entry level is usually the fear man because of insecurity. When this happens, many other fear doors are opened, and life can become filled with all manner of things that bring terror and reinforce insecurity. But the most difficult thing is that it opens us to doubt and lack of trust on a major scale, rendering any attempt to walk by faith absolutely futile.

> "I don't know any parents that look into the eyes of a newborn baby and say, 'How can we screw this kid up?'" - Russell Bishop

Control. Control is necessary for the perfectionist because failure is not an option. This leads to various forms of manipulation and finally to witchcraft. In marriage and family situations it can be expressed as being anywhere from exerting absolute control and domination to passive-aggressive manipulation. We often see one party in a marriage trying to "fix" the other so they'll be happy, as though they had no issues of their own. I believe this is also one of the issues in our current societal experience of young people, who are generally unable to commit to marriage until their biological clock is about to die. Our fatherless society has spawned an entire generation of people who have to be in control of their circumstances in order to ensure themselves that they will not experience pain again. Consequently, they run around trying to manipulate others into being responsible for their happiness. Can you say, "relationship killer"?

> *"The search for a father is a search for authority outside yourself; you feel wraithlike, incomplete without him, in whatever form he takes."* - Nick Lyons

Cautiousness. This is born out of the fear of failure, such that the perfectionist becomes cautious in everything as a means to limiting the risk of failure. It robs the individual of spontaneity and life. Surprises are feared rather than embraced. I knew a person who would, for years, open and re-seal all her Christmas presents so that on Christmas morning she would know how to react before the others. It is also what keeps us from taking a risk to actualize our dreams and finally become and engage in what we were ultimately created for.

"My father would have enjoyed what you have so generously said of me—and my mother would have believed it." - Lyndon B. Johnson

Lack of Trust. Because the parents were deemed "untrustworthy," so are all other authority figures in life: police, employers, pastors, teachers, coaches, etc.. It is responsible for allowing people to only get so close, even in the context of marriage.

Sexual Issues. Typically, this is a perverted attempt to try to experience the closeness and intimacy that could never be experienced in childhood or later in adulthood because our heart is closed to the exposure of relationship. We all medicate our pain in some form or another. Many perfectionist men fall into pornography during their teen years and may suffer with it well into adulthood. Many have had homosexual relationships in an effort to feel loved, only to add another dimension of daily torment to their lives. Perfectionist women usually fall into promiscuity fairly early in life for the same reasons as men, in an attempt to acquire love and intimacy on their own terms.

When individuals come to us for a ministry "intensive" (two to three days of multiple sessions), we ask them to fill out what we lovingly call our "ministry questionnaire from hell." It is twenty-six pages of questions you never wanted anyone to ask, much less have to answer—and certainly wouldn't want anyone to read. One of those questions asks clients to list all those that they've had sex with as preparation for breaking soul ties. About eight or nine years ago we began to notice that if the client was thirty or under there would roughly be an equal number of males and females on that list, regardless of what sex they were. The pervasiveness of the fatherlessness in this generation is enormous. It creates all manner of sexual confusion in children because it is the presence, interaction, and consistent love of the father that fixes a child's sexual identity.

Judgments. These are always present against father and mother and release the very thing they didn't want to come to pass in their lives. Judgments also break another commandment, Exodus 20:12 and Deuteronomy 6:12, *"Honour thy father and thy mother, as the LORD thy God hath commanded thee; that thy days may be prolonged, and that it may go well with thee, in the land which the LORD thy God giveth thee."*

Vows. Vows are also always present against the way they were raised and against the character and behavior of their father and mother, which has initiated behavior that is diametrically opposed to their own desired way of thinking.

Perfectionism. This is rooted in a need to earn that which should be given freely, namely love from a parent, which speaks value to the child. It requires that an exceptionally higher standard of personal achievement be adopted, which literally drives a person. It results in living with a continual level of frustration, fomenting a hot temper, anger, and resentment; it results in a loss of self worth when the exalted self-imposed standard is not met. Perfectionists live with anger toward themselves and toward their circumstances and will potentially blame shift to anything handy.

Critical Spirit. Every perfectionist is always much harder on themselves than on anyone else. It's part of the curse. The problem is that if one cannot find grace for their own failures, they can extend none to others either—even to those who are closest. We finally begin to mellow as we grow older and begin to cut others some slack but reserve none for ourselves. God is not impressed regardless of who we are critical of.

Since we are well acquainted with our own failures and short comings it is easy to give ourselves grief for every place we fell short or could have done better, even if everyone else is praising our efforts.

Rebellion. This is a distorted mechanism entered to gain attention, which generates a type of attention they don't want, yet which drives them deeper into rebellion. It may also be a behavior that was anti-everything their parents were, especially if their parents were totally evil. Once embraced, it becomes anti-everything else, particularly if it involves authority figures in other arenas.

When a child tries with everything within them to gain a father's attention and sees that it is futile, he or she can become what is known as a "disillusioned perfectionist." They either turn to hyper-perfectionism, passive-aggressive manipulation, or to rebellion, all in a final attempt to gain the attention they desire. Anger is also a constant companion.

Rejection. Rejection is closely related to fear of failure and self-hate; it produces a lifestyle of negative expectations of being rejected and the adoption of numerous coping mechanisms in order to avoid it at all costs. It is a major root to deal with in recovery from poor self esteem.

Guilt and Shame. These two run together because the shame entered when the lies were believed, as parental attention and approval could not be achieved. Guilt and another dose of shame was piled on when they unsuccessfully sought other avenues to achieve it. Guilt and shame are present where ever sin is found, including those areas we judge as sinful which are actually not. For perfectionist, self-imposed guilt and shame are found with the inability to meet one's high personal standards and makes them feel as though they've sinned.

Ahab Spirit. This spirit is a passive-aggressive approach to dealing with inter-personal issues, usually employing manipulation and control using emotions, guilt, and condemnation, or the withholding of affection.

See another book which brings more insight into this particular issue in *Defeating Jezebel,* available from the web site www.houseofhealingministries.org, also available through Amazon.com.

Abandonment. This is produced by lack of attention from a parent or being emotionally disconnected from parental love and acceptance, as well as possibly being physically abandoned by one or both parents. It is closely linked with rejection and is generally couched as a lie about the reliability of God and the value of the individual. It too becomes a negative expectation in life which actually prophesies the end result of being abandoned in all relationships—and, ultimately, by God.

Depression. Actually born of being a disappointed perfectionist, depression is simply the stress induced with the inability, over an extended period of time, to please a parent or the failure of performance to produce love, attention, or the acceptance desired of a parent. Believing the lie that nothing positive can or ever will happen to change current circumstances cements the onslaught. Prolonged depression can also alter the balance of chemicals in the body producing a deep, serious, and long-lasting illness requiring medication. Of course, this is not the only possible source of depression. There are numerous other possibilities, including chemical and hormonal imbalances, nerve problems and generational issues, just to name a few. When engaging those with depression, or if you suffer with it yourself, you need to deal with it from the spirit/soul/body point of view, using a holistic approach which may involve professionals from several disciplines.

Suicide. This is the ultimate in selfishness and self-hate, and the life experience of lack of value. Most of us during adolescent years fought with issues of self worth and self-doubt, and satan threw us an occasional thought about ending it all. The majority of the populace rejected it, but many hung on and have done great damage to themselves as a result. The prophet Elijah came to this point in 1 Kings 19 after a short period of fatigue, stress, and pressure, capped with unreasonable fear that drove him into isolation. When someone is alone with their own thoughts for too long, the enemy can convince him or her of just about anything.

Religious Spirit. In the words of John Sanford,*"religion is defined as a man's search for God, man using Bible study, church attendance, good works, ministry, and devotion to try to find and please God . . . many religious people have transferred perfectionism to God. Now they most emphatically have a 'Father' whose 'demands' have to be lived up to! Never mind that God the Father isn't like that at all. He wears the overlay of life with our earthly parents. The great tragedy is that perfectionists persecute those in restful faith."* And this is because they are not busy "doing" but are more content in simply "being."

Escapism or Denial. This is the basis of all dissociation: a means of not having to continually think about the problems facing them which seem to have no resolution. This can be as simple as turning on the TV and tuning everything else out. It can also be: constant immersion in social media, incessant texting, a smart phone that must be constantly attended to, recreational drug or alcohol usage, intense physical activity, food, adrenaline pumping sports, fantasy, or living out life through a vivid imagination. We all live with some level of emotional pain. Jesus guaranteed it (see John 16:33). But only those who have connected with God on a truly intimate level have found a means to regularly dump it.

Romantic Spirit. This is most often times a fleshly behavior of escapism that starts taking steroids. It can become so consuming that the victim often loses touch with reality and the ability to solve simple problems. Men who fall into pornography during their teen years and do not break this habit, often find themselves in the grip of this spirit well into adulthood.

Disease. I personally believe that about 85 percent of the diseases we encounter have their source in spiritual (emotional) issues.

> *"The source of all spiritually rooted disease is the inability to receive love, because love has the power to break rejection and fear."* - Art Mathias (*Biblical Foundations of Freedom*)

I have never dealt with anyone with deep father issues who didn't have at least one of these issues and who have not had to deal with some of them on some level. Some of them have demonic reinforcement. And if abuse was part of childhood, the issues are usually severe.

Every man I've dealt with that had deep father issues also had lower back problems, which magically went away when the problems were resolved.

I have dealt with numerous women with adrenal failure who's issues were also heavily linked to their fathers. Recovery in these instances is much slower because of the grave damage that is done.

I have also successfully dealt with numerous cases of fibromyalgia that had a similar source, although fear was the major culprit.

Of course, this is certainly not an exhaustive list of the things with which a perfectionist could present. Neither is it intended to say that if you or someone you know or someone you are ministering with or to is a perfectionist all these issues will exist. No one is ever the same; we all process differently, and we all come from different backgrounds where we may have learned a few things that help us mature. The problem exists on a continuum.

Overall, it is very important to simply familiarize yourself with the presenting issues, and the truth will emerge. If this is your issue personally, following my mother's advice is a good starting point, *"Honey, if the show fits, wear it."*

Perfectionism Versus Excellence

There is an alternative that is well worth considering when confronting perfectionism because its goal is the achievement of that which is deemed "approved." That option is excellence. The interesting thing about perfectionism and excellence is that if you measure them principally by their individual productivity, you would have to judge that they are effectively the same, although the equity and maturity of the final product may vary in accord with the training and native skill of the producer. On the whole, the finished product of either would be high, and the overall quality and value of each would also be significant. The functionality of both products would also be expected to be superior by comparison. They would appear to be equal in all respects, except for the personal motivation behind each of them. That's what places them miles apart.

Perfectionism, as we have seen, is fundamentally based in fear: fear of failure and striving to be approved by those in authority. Incredibly high personal productivity standards are the hallmark of every perfectionist because failure is not acceptable. It is not acceptable because to fail would allow someone in authority to declare that the one seeking perfection missed the mark, fell short, and was flawed, and perhaps fatally so. The personal drive and commitment to reaching a place where those words could never be spoken is the ultimate goal. The result is that the perfectionist is driven to avoid failure to the point that it consumes them.

Every perfectionist that I have ministered to over the years has universally complained of being emotionally weary, which in due time became physical and emotional exhaustion. It takes an enormous amount of energy to keep all the ducks in a row, all the balls in the air, and all the plates spinning. It is interesting that the more intelligent a person is and the healthier he or she is the longer they can keep it all going, so long as there is some level of emotional maturity to accompany it—otherwise everything begins to fall apart by their mid-to-late thirties causing a pre-mature mid-life crisis. If there is a major crisis with health somewhere in there it will fall apart sooner. Adrenal failure is often one of the results.

It is the drive that eventually steals the joy of achieving. Life then becomes a never-ending treadmill of responsibility. The perfectionist may attempt to turn to close relationships for temporary respite, but they too can only provide so much distraction because the dogged pursuit of legitimacy (being unconditionally accepted for who we are) will not relent at all.

Excellence is the antithesis of perfectionism because it is the God-given result of all the natural motivations of the heart. We naturally want to do our best, we naturally gravitate to improving our knowledge and skill level, and we naturally understand the benefits of maturity in the expression of any discipline. It was built into us when we were created.

When God finished creating the world, what did He do? He surveyed His work and appraised His proficiency, declaring "It is good." He didn't say that it was "above average," nor would He have been satisfied with "it's good enough." Since we were created in His image, we have the same motivation: the joy of creating, the thrill of making something work properly, the satisfaction of solving a problem, and the fulfillment of a job well done.

Perfectionism drives whereas excellence compels. Because perfectionism employs rules and regulations (even if they are of our making), it falls into the same sentence that Paul accorded the law in Romans 7 when he talks about how it produced death in him because he could not live up to it. Excellence, on the other hand, produces life because it compels us to create from our spirit and the depth of our soul, where life comes from.

Choose life!

The Problem of Maintaining Depth of Relationship

Entering into deep personal relationships is perhaps the greatest long term problem for a perfectionist. Because this condition was entered into in a generally unsuccessful attempt to work for that which should have been given freely, a large portion of the heart has been shut down because the pain of the daily rejection from not receiving it was so great. That which was shut down to avoid consciously feeling the pain of rejection doesn't automatically reset itself to wide open when they get introduced to Mr. or Miss Right. When walls and barriers are raised internally in order to keep out the pain, we are totally unmindful of the fact that those walls and barriers are indiscriminate about what they keep out, such that it is as effective in resisting the entrance of love as it is pain.

True intimacy in relationship, then, cannot be guaranteed because the heart will not be totally (completely) open for and to the one to which it is directed. There may be a season in a relationship in which the issue becomes known, but until the process of breaking perfectionism is started, the switch to turn it back on is too hard to find, no matter how hard one tries.

This is not a permanent indictment against the ability of a perfectionist to enter into a healthy, wholesome relationship. All I am saying is that the process necessary to build sufficient trust to allow anyone in is a difficult one that requires both bravery and longevity in the process. It requires taking chances emotionally with people, which may be very difficult to do in large doses. Bottom line: it will take time. Unfortunately, many of a perfectionist's "significant others" may feel that they have waited too long already. So if those relationships are to weather the process, they are going to have to be emotionally engaged in it with until all the habit patterns of the perfectionist's lifestyle are broken.

The key is to get delivered of a demon of self-hate. Then the progress picks up speed.

Risk Aversion

In January 2012, we started a project for thirty-seven people called "Life Launch." It was created to be the answer to an observed problem with a group of people we were connected with. It seemed that many had come to the end of high school without knowing what they wanted to do with their lives and without a specific direction they enrolled in college. They had graduated from college in much the same condition, and without any specific life direction, they chose to enroll in a master's degree program. And here they were again: still clueless. So we put the program together to help them do several things:

1. Help them establish a level of relationship with God in an attempt to get His input regarding what they should do with their lives;
2. Give them specific information which would help each of them understand how they were uniquely formed and fashioned by God to achieve something important in the world;
3. Give them a road map to help them recover the lost and stolen dreams;
4. Help them identify and remove roadblocks to emotional and spiritual health; and
5. Provide them a venue to help them process their way through the maze.

As far as we could tell, the whole affair went swimmingly well for about five months. They were enlightened, invigorated, achieved the needed direction, and recovered their dreams; they even collectively found a new place with the Lord and others were able to begin processing their new-found destinies and purposes in life. The students were even thrilled by what they received. Sounds great, eh?

In retrospect, we've come to realize that there was one flaw—and a major one at that. Only about 12 percent of the group went on to actualize their new-found direction for life. The remainder, despite their discoveries and some new found disciplines, went back to life as usual.

Now, in the personal prayer ministry "business," we are used to some level of non-performers. I stop short of calling it a prayer ministry failure (and not just because of my own perfectionist tendencies) but because in the final analysis the success or failure of what we do together depends entirely on the willingness and the commitment of the "client" to take the bull by the horns and do what has to be done. I can't do it for them.

For the perfectionist, risk avoidance is the name of the game because avoiding risk means avoiding failure. But, at some point, in order to live life, realize dreams and receive fulfillment on any level we have to take chances. I don't know who first spoke it, but I can guarantee you that the old adage "Nothing ventured, nothing gained!" was not spoken by someone with a risk avoidance issue. As a recovering perfectionist, at some point along the line, you are going to come to the conclusion that this is what you're going to do—no matter what happens! In order to make an omelet, you gotta break some eggs.

Consider these lyrics from a song called, "I Will Wait For You," by Mumford & Sons:

So I'll be bold
As well as strong
And use my head alongside my heart
So tame my flesh
And fix my eyes
That tethered mind free from the lies

But I'll kneel down
Wait for now
I'll kneel down
Know my ground

Raise my hands
Paint my spirit gold
And bow my head
Keep my heart slow

Cause I will wait, I will wait for you
And I will wait, I will wait for you
And I will wait, I will wait for you
And I will wait, I will wait for you

    The beauty of this song is that its author apparently recognizes not only the balance between not totally discounting the mind but authentically living from the heart and also the means to get there, i.e. waiting on God.

    Several years ago my wife and I lived in Atlanta and a pastor friend asked me if I would like to go to Asheville, MC with him to check out the area. He had felt that God wanted him to plant a church there. To make a long story short I fell in love with the place and came home to begin inquiring of God if indeed this was His will that we sell the house and move there.

For about six week I heard nothing, which was very confusing because I thought my heart was already there. One might after ministering to someone I sat down in the chair they had just vacated. It was then the Lord surprised me by saying, "*What do you want?*" Well, I didn't have a theological place to put that. I thought that I would ask God what He wanted, He'd tell me and I'd go do it. He reminded me that sons don't think that way, slaves do. So being the intelligent sort that I am I said, "I know this is an important question, so I'll have to get back to you on that."

Ten days later I did get back to God on the answer to His question and it wasn't until sometime later that I realized the great wisdom in His question and my quest for an answer. (There is more on that in another book.) The bottom line of my answer was that I had made up my mind to move. My wife and I made several trips to Asheville and met some wonderful folks there with whom we are still heart connected today.

A few months later my new Asheville friend, David Kula, asked me how the preparations for move were going. I said we still had some loose ends to tie up. That's when he said something totally profound that speaks right to the heart of the subject we're on; "*When your heart is gone, sooner or later your butt has to catch up.*"

For so many of us trying to get all the ducks in a row and all the details worked out is a bit like herding cats. That's the curse of perfectionism. Sooner or later we have to realize that nothing is ever going to work out perfectly. If you have to wait till it's all perfect the window of opportunity will be closed – the season is passed. Issues of the heart are not bound by a to-do list that must be completed. Yes, if you move you might make a mistake. But if you don't move you just might be making the biggest mistake of your life!

See http://www.fatherhood.org/media/consequences-of-father-absence-statistics

Getting To the Root Issue

Fatherhood

I believe that the relationship between a father and a daughter, or a father and a son, is *the* single most powerfully formative relationship on the earth. It is at the heart of what satan hates the most: not only the love and the discourse in the relationship, but also the interchange which takes place as a result of the relationship which has the potential to change history. That's the first of two powerful reasons why this particular relationship is attacked the most.

The second reason satan hates this relationship so much is that this relationship is also the pattern from which we derive all of our basic initial assumptions or "understanding" of who God is—what his character is like and how we can relate to Him before we actually engage Him. It is often those misconceptions projected upon God that have us holding Him at arm's length.

Some History

In prayer ministry, it is always wise to investigate the parent/child relationship. When God was about to shut down communication with man for 400 years (the span of time between the Old and New Testament periods), He couldn't help but speak about this relationship one more time. So the absolute last thing He addressed was the relationship between a Him and His children, *"Behold I will send Elijah the prophet before the great and terrible day of the Lord comes. And he will turn the hearts of the fathers to the children and hearts of the children to the fathers, lest I smite the land with a curse."* (Malachi 4:6).

What was the big deal about? If we look at the relationship between Elijah and Elisha we get a clue. Elijah was walking along and saw this arrogant kid plowing a field, not with one or two bulls but with twelve! Just imagine the size of the plow that's attached to that! This kid apparently had no problem with self confidence. Elijah offers to be his father in the Lord, and Elisha accepts. Over the course of the next several years, Elijah fathers (mentors, teaches, conveys, transmits, imparts, coaches, instructs, guides, communicates, and passes on) Elisha, telling him everything he knows about life in God and the anointing: how to guard it, how to handle it, how to hear the still small voice of God, and about prayer, fasting, tithing, holiness, honor, and humility … and probably about personal hygiene.

> *"And it came to pass, when they were gone over (the Jordan River), that Elijah said unto Elisha, Ask what I shall do for you, before I am taken from you. And Elisha said, I pray, let a double portion of your spirit be upon me. And he said, You have asked a hard thing: nevertheless, if you see me when I am taken, it shall be so unto you; but if not, it shall not be so."* (2 Kings 2:9)

When Elijah came to the end of his days on the earth and was about to be taken into heaven, he went to Elisha and told him he was "fixin' to check out" and asked him what he wanted for an inheritance."

Elisha no doubt pondered the question for a few moments and then responded that he wanted twice the anointing that Elijah had. Elijah was pleased with his response and told him that he would get it if he saw him go . . . In other words, he was telling Elisha that if he was still close to him—in close relationship—then, and only then, would he get what he asked for.

In essence, Elisha was asking for what, in a non-spiritual sense, would be available to a natural first-born son because, culturally speaking, it was customary for the inheritance to be doled out in advance of the death of the parent. And the first-born son was to receive twice what the other children got because it was his duty to take care of his parents during old age—there was recognition of the expenses necessary in the inheritance to be received. Now, although there is no concrete Biblical evidence that this was the first such intense personal mentoring relationship Elijah had, it must be so because culturally this is how such a covenantal relationship would be conducted.

I believe that it's obvious from several perspectives:

1) it's mentioned (inferred) in the Bible;
2) there was obviously a very close relationship that caused Elijah, knowing he was about to leave the earth, to make the offer to Elisha;
3) Elisha obviously felt that he could ask such a thing on the basis of the depth of the relationship he knew they had shared; and
4) Natural children receive natural inheritances. And, therefore, shouldn't spiritual children receive spiritual inheritances, which is precisely what Elisha asked for.

When Elijah was taken up in the chariot of fire, his mantle (a prophetic and actual symbol of office and authority) fell to the ground. Elisha picked it up, walked to the Jordan River, rolled it up, smacked the water, and walked across on dry ground, just as he and Elijah had shortly before. In fact, according to 2 Kings, the miracles worked at Elisha's hand numbered exactly twice those performed by his father in the spirit, Elijah.

The purpose of the close father/child relationship is to produce Godly offspring that carry twice the anointing of the father. If that is carried forward for multiple successive generations, imagine the level of anointing that is carried just ten generations later! But if the relationship is broken with each generation, each successive generation has to start all over again learning to know God, hear His voice, learn how to carry the anointing. Effectively, we have what we all experience today. That's why satan works so hard to break parental/family spiritual relationships.

According to Romans 8:19, *"For the earnest expectation of the creation waits for the revealing of the sons of God."* So now you know what all creation is really waiting for. It is awaiting the reconciliation of successive generations of fathers and sons in such a manner that the spiritual power and authority of the sons, grandsons, and great-grandsons, when released, reverses the curses inflicted upon both man and the earth.

Relationship Pattern

The second reason satan hates this relationship is that this relationship is also the pattern from which we derive all of our "understanding" of who God is, what His character is like, and how we can relate to Him. The difficulty is that for most of us, our pattern was flawed, or, in some cases, we had none at all. When we came to that time in our lives when we encountered an opportunity to enter into relationship with our Creator, our understanding and expectations were flawed. Fortunately, Holy Spirit was able to convince sufficiently of our need that we entered without reservation.

The trouble began as we attempted to grow in the relationship with some peculiar expectations and more than a little trepidation about what He expected of us and how we would be treated in return. As a result, our lives became a lengthy process of outgrowing what we learned during childhood about relationships in general: relationships with parents, then spouses, relationships with authority figures, relationships with our children, relationships with the opposite sex, and relationships with people of differing educational, cultural, and socio-economic backgrounds.

In 1 Corinthians 15:46, Paul states, *"Howbeit that was not first which is spiritual, but that which is natural; and afterward that which is spiritual."* In other words, first the natural *and then* the spiritual. This is a principle that is in force in which our view of God is actually molded by our relationship with our parents and others pre-Christ.

Age Two to Four Years

The father becomes the primary input person from age two to four and adds the second dimension of an individual's formation. Any of us who have raised children fully recognize something radically changes when a child reaches two. When a child hits the age of two, he or she begins to assert himself or herself in an attempt to: a) experiment with and, if possible, establish independence: b) find out who's in control; and c) establish where the boundaries of the world are. This is when the father's role comes to the forefront of development, and his input commences with a phase of loving instruction and discipline.

The father's role is to build into the child that he or she has intrinsic value and worth, especially to parents. He is to create a safe environment where the child can explore and begin to create; get further instruction and demonstration in unconditional love; learn what love is and how it is expressed, valued, and protected; is taught to respect his mother and other adults in authority; is taught to give and receive affection in an appropriate manner; is instructed in exercising self control; and is taught how to interact with siblings and society in general. This is the beginning of the journey in learning his or her parents' values.

"Surely I have stilled and quieted my soul; Like a weaned child with his mother, Like a weaned child is my soul within me." (Psalm 131:2)

In the context of a loving father-child relationship where nurturing occurs, a child naturally, but subconsciously, sees the picture of what a loving God is because *all* the attributes and many behavioral patterns of the natural father are automatically placed as an expected pattern on God. If satan can break or pervert that relationship then all those negative attributes will also be automatically placed on God.

Also, somewhere during this phase the child learns to eat, talk, walk and run, put on clothes, brush teeth, comb hair, throw balls, ride a bicycle, when to share toys, and when to go to sleep. Life patterns begin to be established. As communication grows, they learn to give and receive love in somewhat more formal ways, but to recognize appreciation and acceptance in any form. As the relationship progresses, such things as faith, belief, and hope automatically enter the picture in progressively more tangible ways. It is where the foundations of communication and trust are established; where responsibility is taught; where the parents' core values of hard work, authority and submission, education, honor, respect, honesty, faithfulness, work ethic, friendship, and loyalty begin to be transmitted. It is where a child learns the appropriate way to convey physically expressions of love and affection through touch. And it is where the value of the extended family begins to be realized.

By age five, and certainly by six, a child has begun to develop beyond strictly relating to the world through feelings and emotions into a stage when cognitive reasoning skills are being built. Up until this time, the child is limited to reacting and interacting to everything through emotions. So when things are good, they are very, very good. And when they are bad, they are very, very bad. There seems to be no middle ground. So love and attention are very, very good, and being treated badly and receiving no attention is very, very, very bad.

The positive acts generate an unconditional love in the child which is stronger than death: love *"bears all things, believes all things, hopes all things, endures all things"* (1 Corinthians 13:7). In the eyes of a loving child, the parent is absolutely perfect, bigger than life, and can do no wrong, can say no wrong, and has power over all things evil in the universe ... and is absolutely trustworthy. According to Proverbs 10:12, *"Hatred stirs up strife: but love covers all sins."*

If a child is reared in an environment bereft of positive, nurturing parental attention, low self esteem issues are significant. If abuse is part of the equation, we find that the individual's ability to both receive love, and give love, is seriously impaired, if not absolutely non-functional. Because the "landing pad for incoming affirmation" has not been constructed by the parents, they are not even capable of receiving a compliment because the "personal value" receptor is broken.

Fear of rejection is number one on the list. Because they do not love themselves, they in turn cannot live in true love and therefore experience significant fear and trust issues with everyone. They expect to be rejected because they feel they have nothing of value within them that qualifies them as being loveable or acceptable. They may become manipulators of others in a continuously aborted effort to obtain the love and acceptance they desire so badly. Others become passive-aggressive manipulators in an attempt to forcibly pull what they need from others. Understanding the general characteristics of birth order personalities is often helpful in getting to the root issue.

"My son, hear the commands of your father, And forsake not the instruction of your mother." (Proverbs 1:8)

When a young child (four and under) is abused, the previous assessment of the parent by the child still does not change as love covers a multitude of sin. It's true whether you're a believer or not. If what a child experiences feels bad or hurts, or both, somebody has to be wrong. In order for the equation to work, the child must change his view of himself; satan is ever present to help them "mis-understand" what's going on and feeds them a lie that places the blame for all the negative parental behavior squarely on them. So they are presented with a "truth" about the situation which says since what is happening to me is bad I must somehow deserve it so I am a bad person. Therefore, the child takes the blame for all the parent's anger, frustration, bad behavior, and abuse, whether physical, sexual, or mental.

Once the lie is adopted, the adult cannot escape it any more than the child could. Their "truth" now becomes *the truth*. The adult then believes that he or she is not worthy of love, success, or anything else. They will always settle for second best in love and life because that's what the bitter root expectations dictate And even when they day-dream (which they can consciously control), it is always filled with visions of personal loss and failure.

It is also natural for a child to believe everything that the ultimate authority figure (a parent) says, and particularly a father, even if they are absolute lies. If a parent verbally berates and abuses a child for an extended period of time, the child often believes they have no worth, no value, and are incapable of being able to do what everybody else does. After all, parents don't lie so what they say, even in anger, must be true. Adult perfectionists often live in a constant state of mild frustration, confusion, and anger and are sometimes rendered incapable of making quick decisions, have difficulty establishing near term priorities, and may have a poor memory because all the parameters have to be filtered through the question of "will this get me the love, attention, and value that I need, and is there risk of failure?"

As was the case with me, my father was not abusive. He was not even relationally dysfunctional—a little stiff maybe but not to dysfunctional. He was just totally absent. It is the same when divorce or death ravages the home of a child. In all these cases, satan comes to sow lies and help us misinterpret every event. He finds fertile soil in the heart of a hurting child who has been robbed of unconditional love and acceptance. He tells the child that if he or she were better the parent wouldn't have left. And on, and on, because there is no one there to refute them. They are accepted as truth, and a destructive mentality is born.

When a child from such a background becomes an adult two things happen: all those lies and the positive and negative attributes and characteristics of the natural father are automatically superimposed upon God and upon every authority figure. An example of the unconscious thought process is the following: "If I had to earn my father's love and attention as a child, maybe I can earn God's love and attention; working sixty hours a week proves that I am a conscientious and loyal employee." Everything in the Christian life is then seen through the colored glasses of performance. Entire passages of Scripture and basic fundamental concepts of the faith like grace and unconditional love hold no personal meaning beyond terms which have definitions assented to intellectually.

They are imprisoned between a rock and a hard place. Every Sunday they hear that they need God's approval to get to Heaven, and they strive all week to get it, subconsciously hating the treadmill it binds them to and never understanding or accepting that it is a free gift through Jesus Christ. This is because their "truth" is that acceptance and approval are earned—and there is no other truth. They can repeat for you the message preached to them, but it all comes out of the head because their heart still believes that they must perform.

In time, they begin to formulate a view that says "my identity is what I do." Many stricken with perfectionism, and its smaller brother performance-orientation, often define themselves by their career or job title. They will never introduce themselves as, "I work as a . . ." or "my job is . . .," but they always identify themselves as "Hi, *I'm* a lawyer" or "*I am* a . . . whatever their title is." When they get depressed, they remind themselves of their career accomplishments.

At some point, however, frustration sets in. As hard as it is to try to achieve intimacy with God, they are seemingly no closer than when they first started. When hope begins to fade, they are faced with the choice of plodding on in hopes that somehow and some day and in some way they can break through, or they simply give up the active seeking and stick with what they've got, no matter how unsatisfying it may be. With resignation, hope of ever living the abundant life fades away along with all the other broken dreams of happiness. Oddly enough, the paradigm is so strong that very few people get *consciously* angry with God. They may be given to questioning why He isn't more proactive on their behalf, but they generally never allow it to build beyond that.

My wife and I dealt with a young lady recently in a ministry session that dealt with some very heavy issues. She had lived on the street since she was 15 and had been a prostitute for eight years in order to survive. When told that she was now free to dream she said, "I don't think I know how. All my dreams have been to get through what was going on at the time ... and that was really just wishing."

Adopting the real truth is the only hope for escape from bondage and entry into freedom. In these cases, one or more inner healing sessions with an anointed brother or sister is the prescribed method for getting to the root issue.

Once discovered and properly dealt with, freedom comes rather quickly. It is the lies that take some time to uproot – one must re-learn how to live.

The real power behind inner healing is that although the memories of traumatic events remain, they no longer have any emotional power to them. So a reverie no longer has the power to produce pain. Once the power to produce or recall emotional pain has been eliminated, a once powerful memory of a terrible event can rest alongside an equally happy memory without producing turmoil. This is how the Apostle Paul could say, "*. . . let the past be the past, and reach forward to the high calling of God in Christ Jesus*" (Philippians 3:13). When inner healing is accomplished, the past no longer has power to dictate the future.

Once free, one must stay free. And in order to stay free, one must "renew" his or her mind with the Word of God (see Romans 12:2), so that the individual is "walking in the Spirit" and not according to learned habit patterns created by natural coping mechanisms. Once the truth is known, the truth will set them free from ever coming under the domination of demonic spirits again (see John 8:32).

This is best accomplished in the context of community where one has multiple life-giving relationships that promote truth, encouragement and instruction. Very few of us have access to three individuals who can provide for those functions in our lives. But this is precisely what God would like to provide for us. Start praying for those specific resources. They are out there.

Breaking the Curse of Perfectionism

My experience has been that defeating this thing is at least a five (5) step process;

a) Repenting for agreeing with the system of perfectionism – the way of the world.
b) Deliverance from a spirit of self-hate.
c) Identifying all the habit patterns and mindsets that have been adopted which define the individual's world view and the current methodology of processing information and events.
d) Re-building a fully relational life based on intentional interaction with all the members of a local community.
e) Establishing a relationship with God based on son-ship or daughter-ship rather than the duty of a slave.

Typically, once diagnosed I begin to deal with the curse of perfectionism using Lehman's set of birth order characteristics. If you put on your spiritual glasses you will find that it pretty well describes all the issues that have to be dealt with. (Understand; These characteristics will become strengths when submitted to God and become mature. They are weaknesses when under the ruler of this world.)

To review: First-born and Only children (because they share so many characteristics) can generally be described as;

Perfectionists, reliable, conscientious, list makers, well-organized, hard-driving, natural leaders, critical, serious, scholarly, individuals who don't like surprises, and people who love computers; an Only child can generally be described as a little adult by age seven, very thorough, deliberate, a high achiever, self-motivated, fearful, someone who can't bear to fail, having very high expectations for self, and being more comfortable with people who are older or younger.

As you pray a repeat-after-me prayer of repentance to dismantle the spiritual aspects/effects of the "way of the world," you should follow a particular order as you address each issue . . .

Perfectionism. Typically, we know whether or not there is enough evidence to convict us of being a perfectionist. And if we're ever clueless, we can always rely on our good friends to tell us if we qualify, generally with a significant degree of accuracy. This is the way of the world. On some level, we were taught it by our parents, caught it from them if they too were perfectionists, or had tendencies in that direction because: it's taught in every school, it's part of every athletic program, and it's part of every business endeavor. As a result of agreement with it, perfectionism quickly becomes more than just a way of life, and it governs all of life. It's how we see, process, and respond to everything in our world. It becomes part of our iniquitous belief system (along with all our family junk), and we pass it on to our kids. It is absolutely insidious, and there is not one area of our lives that it will not invade.

Breaking its hold in our lives requires us to repent of adopting it, believing in its power to save us from pain, relying on it to defend us from being "found out," and agreeing with it. Then we have to ask the Lord to show us every habit pattern, every paradigm of thought, and every nuance of ideology that agrees with perfectionism.

Laws, Rules, and Regulations. Once perfectionism is adopted, we begin to amass a whole series of laws, rules, and regulations that tell us how to live life. More importantly, all these laws, rules, and regulations we collect along the way are what we adopt as those that will ensure success, avoid failure, and manage all the risks. But these are not ordinary rules. These are perfect rules and must be followed to the letter in order to produce the desired effect: success, which we automatically reframe as personal value.

The Apostle Paul wrote about this specifically in Romans 7:1, "*Know ye not, brethren, (for I speak to them that know the law), how that the law hath dominion over a man as long as he liveth?*" In other words, Paul came to realize that all those laws, rules, and regulations he could neither remember, nor keep completely, produced nothing but death in him.

So it is with us. In order to keep all these self-acquired laws, rules, and regulations, we must live life through our heads and not in accord with Romans 8:2 (life in the Spirit).

When perfectionism is fully embraced, life is lived predominately through our brain rather than our heart because that's what hurts, and avoiding hurt is the whole reason for perfectionism. Consequently, there are several reasons to break perfectionism.

Critical. The primary problem with agreeing with perfectionism is dependent upon what stage of life the perfectionist is in, being either old enough to begin to grant other people grace for making mistakes or somewhere in the process of learning to do so. Early on, the granting of grace is refused due to pride and the belief that the adopted laws, rules, and regulations are *the* laws, rules, and regulations that should be lived out by everyone. So everybody else has the problems!

Judgments always produce exactly what isn't wanted. Matthew 7:1-3 says, *"Judge not, that ye be not judged. For with what judgment ye judge, ye shall be judged: and with what measure ye mete, it shall be measured to you again. And why beholdest thou the mote that is in thy brother's eye, but considerest not the beam that is in thine own eye?"* In other words, what goes around comes around, and trying to avoid problems actually draws them.

For perfectionists, problems equate to failure and that just be! In an attempt to avoid problems, perfectionists must analyze every activity. As a matter of course, a perfectionist knows precisely where and what could have been done better, how it could have been improved upon, and where they narrowly missed failing. The self-criticism never ends, and they will never grant themselves grace in the process. Consequently, if a perfectionist does mess up, the self-imposed guilt, shame, and condemnation will also never end. The bottom line is that perfectionism requires that a person comes under the subjugation of a critical spirit. This is something that must be addressed specifically.

More Comfortable with People Older or Younger. This is the case because a perfectionist can freely associate with those who have not yet learned to judge (younger) and those who have given it up (older). It's the peers that are deemed to be a problem.

List maker. Being a list maker is just one more way of describing one who has bought into to fear of failure. Perfectionism requires, in this area, that a perfectionist comes under the subjugation of spirit of fear. This is also something that must be addressed specifically.

Conscientious and Reliable. As a perfectionist, being conscientious is simply code for agreeing with a spirit of fear, specifically the fear of man. Because he or she is 1fearful of not pleasing someone, or many, a perfectionist is a stickler for keeping promises, remembering dates, and executing responsibilities with precision. This, too, is something that must be addressed specifically because if there is one thing that consistently wars against the characteristics of conscientiousness and reliability it is procrastination. And procrastination is directly linked to the fear of failure and is most often found among perfectionists.

Serious and Well-organized. It takes a great deal of concentration, energy, and effort to keep all the balls in the air, all the plates spinning, and all the ducks in a row. One of the first things to suffer is a perfectionist's sense of humor. They cannot afford to be laughed at, or with, because it means there's been a failure or something to be embarrassed about. That equates to personal failure and that cannot be allowed to happen under any circumstance. So to laugh at oneself is not allowed. This will require repentance for voluntarily allowing the enemy to steal all the joy from life—the very thing Jesus came to give us (see John 10:10).

Doesn't Like Surprises and Loves Computers. These two characteristics are closely related to the fear of failure. Surprises mean that there's been a failure in planning, or a lack of attention to detail and a serious deficit of control. That means inherent in a surprise is an unprogrammed response to something unexpected, which has the potential for failure in it. (Remember, failing at something is equated by a perfectionist as being a failure personally, and being a failure means that there is actually a major defect in the person and it probably can't be fixed and, therefore, success is permanently out of reach. So there must never be a failure. It cannot be allowed!) And computers are absolutely predictable; they are always precise and are paragons of correctness. Unless there's a virus, they will do exactly what you tell them to do and do it well—nothing more or less. They are the perfectionist's dream.

Hard Driving and a Natural Leader. Statistics do not lie. Two-thirds of all of our US presidents are first-born sons, about 81 percent of all generals in the military are the first born, and approximately 70 percent of all major inventions in the last 100 years were by first-born children. That is because the children born first born are driven to succeed and have the ability to draw those around. This drive can obviously be good or bad depending upon the endeavor that they choose. It also means that when things go into the ditch, the drive will cause them to be irretrievably driven into the ditch.

Scholarly. This characteristic is made up of both curiosity and failure avoidance, although the latter is out weighted by the former. The aspect of curiosity is that which feeds vision and expands personal horizons. Most first-born children experience a life-long quest for knowledge that is not limited to a single interest. It is also that which ultimately contributes significantly to their success in life—

and is major factor in their natural ability to lead people. Like anything else, it can be overdone.

The Prayer to Break Perfectionism

To break the curse of perfectionism repenting for decisions made that caused it to be adopted in the first place is necessary. To that end, I have crafted a prayer. Before praying, however, there are a few important things to consider.

The first thing that must be broken is the hold that perfectionism has. There is a need for repenting for agreeing with the system of this world and taking on its values, as well as relying on it to protect from further pain and gain a sense of worth.

Perfectionists have set up a whole series of rules and behavioral expectations for themselves in order to gain approval and value. They are much stricter than the world at large, or even the most rigid religious sect. They must voluntarily lay down all these rules, regulations, and standards that have been set up as their laws of life—the rules and regulations that determine how to achieve success, avoid failure, and manage the risk. They must lay down their rules and regulations because they are the laws of death, not of life. They must lay down their rules and regulations that define how life is supposed to function, not how it actually operates. They must lay down their rules and regulations that attempt to predetermine how to earn joy, not how to live it. And then they must choose to walk in accord with the law of life in Christ Jesus (see Romans 8:2).

They also need to verbally agree to cut themselves some slack and give themselves permission to fail and not measure up to everybody's expectations. They need to give themselves permission to be human! Since they are never going to achieve their goal of personal perfection, they must give themselves permission to make mistakes.

They must break agreements with a critical spirit, one that led them down a path of guilt, shame, and self-condemnation. They must then forgive themselves for putting up the standards that couldn't be met, and for continually putting themselves down for not being able to meet them. They have to cut off all residual self-imposed guilt and shame. And then they must choose to grant themselves the same grace that they grant to total strangers.

They need to ask the Lord's forgiveness for voluntarily giving up their joy and their self-esteem and for believing the lies of the enemy rather than what God says about them.

Then they need to ask God's forgiveness for believing lies and making judgments about themselves. They should make a list of them if possible, which will undoubtedly contain all manner of lies about God's creation and how they have judged His creation as not being worthy. They need to ask His forgiveness for believing lies about God and His desire and ability to love His creation.

They should read and expound upon Psalm 139 to help jump start their thinking, putting their name in several spots and then meditating on the passage as a way of renewing how they think about themselves and the way God really views them.

Here is my version of this "repeat-after-me prayer":

Father, in the name of Your son Jesus Christ, I ask Your forgiveness for coming into agreement with the system of this world, the teachings of the enemy himself, and for adopting his values and his system of weights and measures. I repent for making myself the god of my own world and believing that I could control my circumstances and dictate my own outcomes. Forgive me!

In the mighty name of Jesus, on behalf of myself and my entire blood line, I break, shatter, cut off, and destroy all agreement with perfectionism and the system of this world. On behalf of myself and my family line, I renounce its teachings, its principles, its rules and regulations, and any of its authority in my life and those of my family members. I ask You, Father, to break any and all curses from me and from my generational line that were established because of our agreement and participation with this iniquitous system.

I ask You, Father, to disconnect me and my family line from any demonic entities that have been assigned to us as a result of our repeated agreement with the system of the enemy. Will You also cancel any demonic strategies that have been planned against us to hold us in this place?

As an act of my will, I renounce and lay down all the rules and regulations that I have amassed over the years that have determined how to achieve success, avoid failure, and manage the risk of potential failure. I choose to no longer live by slavery to the law and its curses, even if it is ones I created. In Jesus' name, by the power of the Holy Spirit, I choose to now live by the law of life in Christ Jesus. I ask that You show me every habit pattern that I have created that is built upon the perfectionist system I just resigned from and grant me the grace to establish new habit patterns that are Kingdom-oriented.

I ask you to show me every belief system, every paradigm of thought, every portion of my world view that agrees with the system of the enemy. I choose to open my eyes to what you show me and I ask that you grant me insight into every principle that I have adopted. I ask that you grant me the grace to make different decisions, all of which agree with the precepts of your Word.

I ask your forgiveness where I have been so bold as to establish my own values, my own understanding of "right and wrong" that accommodated my flesh and my self-will. I willfully declare that you are right and I am wrong. Teach me your ways.

Henceforth, I choose to grant myself the grace to fail, to not get it right, to make mistakes. I loose myself from fear of failure and renounce any allegiance I had to that spirit and its rule over me. I take that ground back and I give to the Lord Jesus Christ for Him to rule and reign over.

I break, shatter, cut off, and destroy all allegiance to a critical sprit. I command you to go from me now. I ask, Father, that You restore to me the Spirit of Joy that I gave up when I embraced this ungodly system. I ask that You restore my sense of humor, and the ability to laugh at my own mistakes, and to not take myself so seriously. Teach me how to play again. I choose to live free of self-condemnation and self-imposed guilt and shame. I will no longer accuse and abuse myself by continually rehearsing where I blew it, where I could have done better, or where I made a mistake. As your Word declares to me, "Life and death are in the power of the tongue" (Proverbs 18:21). I will henceforth guard my mouth so that I continually speak only life (see Deuteronomy 30:19 over myself and my affairs.

I break, shatter, cut off, and destroy all allegiance to a spirit of self-hate. I command you to go from me now. I repent for agreeing with the enemy that I was not worthy, not valuable, not loveable. I choose to agree with You, Father, that what You made was good. Forgive me for thinking otherwise. I also choose to believe what You say about me, above what I have been taught or learned while under that system.

I choose to forgive my father and mother, and any other authority figure in my life, for disappointing me, for not treating me as I thought they should, even for abusing and mistreating me. I forgive them for not accepting me as the gift I was to them; for not accepting me as was, for using me as though I was property to do with as they pleased. I ask You, Father, to forgive them as well. I repent for any judgments that I made against them and cancel any vows that I made that said I would not be like them in any way, nor model their behavior. I ask Your forgiveness for dishonoring them.

I ask Your forgiveness for shutting down my heart and believing that I could defend myself from experiencing more heart ache on my own terms. Forgive me for taking matters into my own hands rather than depending upon the power of Your Spirit to heal and nurture. I choose to once again open my heart to live.

Father, where I have shut down my ear to You and damaged my ability to walk in all You created me for by dependence upon myself, I repent and ask You to restore me to full functionality once again. I ask You to restore any damage done to any portion of my body while I was under the spell cast by this system. I ask You to once again draw the line between my natural mind and its instincts of self preservation and my spirit, so that I may quickly discern the difference between what is Your way and those of my own devices.

I ask You, Father, to restore to me the blessings of my family line that I and my family have forgone as a result of participating with this system. If there are any purposes that You had in Your heart for me and my family line to achieve that were thwarted by our allegiance to the system of the world, I ask that You renew them, call them forward, and I ask that you grant us the grace and impart whatever gifting is necessary to complete them, that nothing would you desired would remain unaccomplished by me or my family line.

Father, I thank You for hearing my prayer."

This prayer will go a long way toward dealing a death blow to this issue. The next phase is walking it out. And that's a bit more difficult because old habits die hard and auto-response mechanisms to self-protect are strong. It will take a bit more work to uproot them all.

There are two things that will help along the way, however: accountability and a prayer partner. They may be one in the same, but an accountability partner is one to whom permission is given to be nosey regarding how the perfectionist is doing in the midst of the process, as well as to be brutal in the questioning. He or she is definitely the most useful of the two while in this process. The goal is two-fold: find both and get connected . . . and stay connected.

I would also recommend a few additional books. One of the most problematic aspects of perfectionism is recovering from the damage done through self-hate. It takes time to heal those wounds. The process can be accelerated by intentionally pressing into the places that the perfectionist least wants to go—into the heart of the Father. To that end, Jack Frost has written two books about his own journey: *Experiencing Father's Embrace* and *Spiritual Slavery to Spiritual Sonship* (both available through either www.shilohplace.org or Amazon.com).

If you, or the perfectionist to whom you are ministering, is not in a church that either has a healing community integral to it, or has one the is at least connected to it, find one and attend it regularly.

If you came out of a church background like mine, church is about the last place you want to be. Church isn't the point. It's regularly putting yourself in an environment in which you have given God freedom to operate that's the point. For some reason He delights in breaking in on you when you least expect it. I don't know why, but He seemed to love to do it when I was serving as an usher back when I was starting to work through my "father issues." I would be in the back of the sanctuary during worship trying to participate without being noticed, when suddenly He would envelope me in His unmistakable presence. I would be totally overwhelmed. It wasn't a frequent occurrence, but it was frequent enough that after a while I sort of half-expected it to happen again.

Each time it happened I noticed my freedom had been advanced somehow. I could sense it. I knew something had been done but had no idea what He had done. And I don't have a clue how He does it or why He chooses to do it when He does either. All I know is that when He shows up, things change for the better. So my advice is to intentionally put yourself in a place where He can encounter you regularly.

If there is a small group that functions as part of that healing community, particularly if it can help you process through parental issues, join it. Every step you choose to take toward healing will put you one step closer to walking in the fullness of life that Jesus died for you to have.

Fit For the Kingdom of God

This treatise would not be complete without touching again on the initial question raised by the rich young ruler in Matthew 19, but viewed from another perspective. In his response, Jesus was at once speaking to the ultimate pursuit of the perfectionist soul: being perfect in the eyes of man and being perfectly fit for the Kingdom of God.

The response of Jesus in verse 21, "*If you would be perfect...*" was surely a response for the ages because Jesus was not only responding to the way things were under the current covenant, but he was also highlighting how they were going to become under the new covenant ratified in His own blood.

Relationship

The first thing Jesus wanted to point out was that the Kingdom of God is based solely in relationship. Further, that relationship with others was on the same level as relationship with God. I think that it is interesting that the cross upon which Jesus died is made up of two beams: one vertical and one horizontal, indicating the power of redemption for relationship restored between God and man and between men. Consequently, the reference to keeping those specific commandments had everything to do with the importance of restoration/maintenance of relationship between and among men, for those commandments dictated how we are to treat everyone else. They became the foundational building blocks of moral law upon which "most" of our modern day laws are based.

Several years ago my wife and I had a number of twenty-some-things troupe into our office fearful that they "were missing their destiny." It is a fearsome thing to consider that you might actually be missing the very reason God purposed in His heart (before the foundation of the world) for you here on the earth. It is highly unlikely that would happen for someone in their late teens, but logically it is certainly possible and therefore not a thought to be dismissed lightly. I decided to look into it.

I thought that a Word study would produce some results, so I went to Scripture and looked up all the verses with the word "destiny" or its derivatives in them and found that there are very few. Those that did essentially said the same thing . . . you are destined to become conformed to the image of Jesus Christ. Checking through Hebrew origins, I found that the word translated as "destiny" could just as well have been translated "fate." In other words, once you become a believer in Jesus Christ you will become transformed/conformed into the image of Jesus Christ—no doubt about it! I am certain that there are things you can do to drag out the process, but once you've given your heart to Jesus and His spirit comes to dwell in you, the fine print in the contract to which you verbally agreed takes full and complete effect.

Not fully convinced that this was the destiny the youngsters were afraid of missing, I searched for other more destiny-like verses. I settled on Ephesians 2:10, *"There are good works established for you to perform before the foundation of the world."* Now, that sounded like a destiny verse if ever I heard one!

I then moved on to see if I could find out what those spine-chilling, headline-making, world-changing, good works were that, when accomplished, would forever fix our names in lights in the halls of heaven. Surely this list of miracles to be done would be a great list to wave before those stuck in mundane doldrums of everyday life and would fulfill everyone's secret desire to be like Elijah and Elisha!

What I found surprised me. Here's the list of good works prepared for us before the foundation of the world:

> Love God.
> Love others as yourself.
> Honor your parents.
> Love your spouse.
> Raise your children in the ways of the Lord.
> Treat your bosses and employees with honor.
> Be honest (don't lie or steal).
> If you get angry, handle it in a Godly manner.
> Be faithful in what you promise.
> Keep others' interests above your own.
> Love your enemies.

I have to tell you I struggled with this revelation. I was studied a bit more on this topic and came to John 15:12, *"A new commandment I give you, love one another, even as I loved you"* and Romans 13:10, *"Love works no ill to his neighbour: love therefore is the fulfillment of the law."*

I also stumbled on to something else . . . 'perfection' was actually mentioned frequently in the Bible as well, but not in the context that I had used to seeing it . . .

"... and above all these things put on love, <u>which is the bond of perfectness</u>." (Colossians 3:14)

"Howbeit <u>we speak wisdom among the perfect</u>: yet a wisdom not of this world, nor of the rulers of this world, which are coming to nought." (1Corinthians 2:6)

"Being confident of this very thing, that he which began a good work in you <u>will perfect it</u> until the day of Jesus Christ." (Philippians 1:6) "Let us therefore, as many as be perfect, be thus minded: and if in anything ye are otherwise inded, even this shall God reveal unto you." (Philippians 3:15)

"To whom God was pleased to make known what is the riches of the glory of this mystery among the Gentiles, which is Christ in you, the hope of glory: whom we proclaim, admonishing every man and teaching every man in all wisdom, that we may present every man perfect in Christ; whereunto I labour also, striving according to his working, which worketh in me mightily." (Colossians 1:27-29)

"And these all, having had witness borne to them through their faith, received not the promise, 40 God having provided some better thing concerning us, <u>that apart from us they should not be made perfect</u>." (Hebrews 11:39-40)

"But ye are come unto mount Zion, and unto the city of the living God, the heavenly Jerusalem, and to innumerable hosts of angels, to the general assembly and church of the firstborn who are enrolled in heaven, and to God the Judge of all, and to the spirits of <u>just</u>

men made perfect, and to Jesus the mediator of a new covenant." (Hebrews 12:22-24)

"Now the God of peace, who brought again from the dead the great shepherd of the sheep with the blood of the eternal covenant, even our Lord Jesus, 21 make you perfect in every good thing to do his will, working in us that which is well–pleasing in his sight, through Jesus Christ; to whom be the glory forever and ever. Amen." (Hebrews 13:20-21)

"There is no fear in love: but perfect love casteth out fear, because fear hath punishment; and he that feareth is not made perfect in love." (1 John 4:18)

You are free to draw your own conclusions, but I think the implication is clear: there exists an achievable perfection for each of us that does not require hard demanding work, burdensome toil, and striving (see Hebrews 4:9-12). It is the embracing of the Lord Jesus Christ as both savior and Lord of your life. Being made perfect then, is both an event and a process. Positionally, because of our faith in God through Jesus, we are made perfect in our human spirit, where the Holy Spirit has taken up residence, while we also enter into a process of being conformed to His image in our soul (see Philippians 1:6 above). This why we have to "work out our salvation."

Hebrews 4:9-12 states that we must choose to enter into the rest of the Lord, a process of learning to cease from our striving to be perfect through the continual application of the strength of our own arm, so that we may learn to allow Him to do it effortlessly as we cooperate with Him.

It is interesting how those in areas where our natural father was able to build into us what he should have we seem to have very little problem allowing God to do His thing in those areas. But where our natural father did not plant, water, and cultivate in us what was needed, our basic ability to trust in those areas is such that we never freely allow God a free hand. It's always a fight.

My prayer is that as you bring perfectionism to death in your life, and those with whom and to whom you may minister, you would be able to easily allow the Holy Spirit to finish the work in you so that the fullness of the Kingdom of God may be expressed in you and through you to the balance of creation. It needs it!

Made in the USA
San Bernardino, CA
18 September 2015